God Loves Me So

To Erlene
Gods blessings
and joy always

Evelyn McCarthy

God Loves Me So

Evelyn McCarthy

A Division of WINEPRESS PUBLISHING

Pleasant Word (a division of WinePress Publishing, PO Box 428, Enumclaw, WA 98022) functions only as book publisher. As such, the ultimate design, content, editorial accuracy, and views expressed or implied in this work are those of the author.

ISBN 1-4141-0636-X
Library of Congress Catalog Card Number: 2005910350

Dedication

This book is dedicated to my daughter Camille Scott, who has walked with me through all the years of putting the book together, laughing, saying, "You can do it," and believing in me.

To my other five children who also supported and encouraged me: Patrick, Thomas, Kenneth, Mary Evelyn Daniels, and Julia Guill. To my brother Charles Emery, who has always been a special part of my life.

Also to Rev. J. Michael Mullin, who stretched me, challenged me, encouraged me, and taught me much in my walk with Jesus throughout these exciting years.

Contents

Foreword

The way people come to faith in Jesus is both predictable and unique. No two persons will travel the exact same road. No two will have the exact same gifts. Yet all who come to maturity in Christ have several things in common. Evelyn's story demonstrates how scripture, advice from fellow Christians, and leading by the Holy Spirit have jointly formed her faith. Add to that a unique sense of the Spirit speaking through her written thoughts, and you have this wonderful story of maturing faith in action.

Many persons never feel prepared to teach a class or organize a city-wide prayer ministry, seeking rather to gain more knowledge. Evelyn takes action as soon as she gets the next piece of the puzzle. Trusting that God will direct her every step, she utilizes the lesson of the day to move into ministry. For some this would be a rush into foolishness, but Evelyn's story is balanced. Rather like Gideon who used a fleece to check out God's direction, she checks to be sure the answer she hears squares with Scripture and with the wisdom of others. It is this careful questioning and equally careful listening that distinguishes Evelyn's growth in faith, keeping it on track and making her exceedingly useful to the Kingdom.

It is easy to fall into error or even fanaticism in religion. Evelyn shares her growth in faith as a model for how to truly hear God and become mature. It is my hope that her story will stimulate many others to listen more closely for the Spirit's leading and to take up the unique task of ministry to which each is called.

J. Michael Mullin
Evelyn's Pastor

Acknowledgments

To my prayer partner, Bettilee Perkins, who has faithfully prayed with me through getting this in print.

To Nancy Matthews for editing my final draft.

To Rev. J. Michael Mullen for editing appropriate theological statements.

To the Texas Prayer Group of The Church of the Epiphany in Dallas, Texas, who prayed for my personal relationship with Jesus Christ so many years ago.

To the many Christian authors whose books I read which encouraged me and helped me to continue my search and understanding of God's love for me.

God Loves Me So

Believe God, let God, in all His majesty,
fill you with the fullness of His love.

Feel the wind of His Spirit blowing on your face, softly, gently. Feel His love, feel His power flowing through you like a sparkling, glistening river. Allow yourself to become immersed in that river of love, that river of life.

This book is to be a fresh wind blowing into the hearts of people.

For God controls the wind of the spirit; when and where He wants it to fall onto the face and into the hearts of the people, it will.

By Evelyn McCarthy

I have struggled for quite some time to actually write this book, because I just did not know where to start. Who am I to write? Does anyone know Evelyn? What credentials do I have? None. Yet over and over, thoughts come and I jot them down. I have journaled many of my experiences and thoughts over the last eighteen years. I believe I am being nudged to write this book. So with much trust in being guided by the Holy Spirit, I have decided to do the best I can. I have struggled with writing this for almost seven years. I began writing it in 1997, and it has taken me into the year 2004 to complete it. One would think it must be a fantastic tome of information. But actually it is just an account of how God has influenced my life. It covers my explanations and understanding of lots of Christian jargon that confronted me in my early exposure to being a new Christian. There are areas of teaching and sharing about how I came to understand what living for Jesus Christ means. I want to assure the reader that I do not have all the answers. I have tried my best to just give you an accounting of how I have questioned and learned and trusted—and not trusted—God for all He is. I will go back to when it all seemed to start.

CHAPTER 1

The Beginning: 1979

I am sitting in this big, ornate church. There are many stained glass windows and lots of statues. I look around and see that one of the windows depicts a person with an outstretched hand that has six fingers. I look at that and think, "Even the stained glass windows are wrong. I can't stand to be here." I want to get up, scream "You are all wrong. What do you really believe? Why are you really here?" and then run out. But I sit there. My hands feel sweaty, and I take big gulps of air. What is wrong with me? Why do I feel this way? I cannot stand to be in a church any longer, whether it is a church I am visiting or the church where I have been a member for all my adult years. There is anger or fear or something inside of me that keeps building up and building up. And it is not just this church or just this day. This particular church is not of my professed denomination, and I grudgingly came today to support my husband in his desire to attend this special service.

Sometimes as I walk across a street, I think, "What if I died right now? What would happen to me? Is there really a God? What is eternity like, if there really is an eternity? What is forever like, and how would I feel knowing I was living with no end to time?" Chills run through me. There is a knot in my stomach. The unknown seems to overwhelm me. I feel my heart racing. I can't stand this. So again, I close down my thoughts. These feelings are coming more frequently. Yet there doesn't seem to be any answers. I don't even want to speak to the people around me at the church I attend. I feel very alone, withdrawn from all that is going on in the church. I decide to quit attending church for awhile. This is a big decision as I have faithfully attended church almost every Sunday since I was sixteen.

Since making the decision to stay away from church, my days all seemed to flow into one big vacuum. On the surface everything was great, but inside I was a mess. I could not tell anyone what I was feeling. Who would understand? Have you been there? A place where you believe no one else could possibly understand, even if you tried to explain. Knowing that the more you tried to explain the worse it would sound, the more confusing it would become.

Most days I blocked out those questioning fears, but every so often they would come to the surface and I would start the wondering process all over again.

The aloneness. The world is full of people, and yet I felt so alone. I would look at a group laughing, sharing, and felt completely alone, as if I were not even there. But did I feel saddened by this? No. I built up a wall. I told myself I didn't need people. I could handle everything. I was in control. After all, I had my husband, my children, my mom, my brother, my friends; I didn't need anyone else. Yet even with them there was a wall. They could only get so far before I shut them out. Why do we do this? Sometimes I thought what a great actress I must be. So many people told me how competent I was, how organized I was, how much talent I had in many areas, what an exciting life I led. Hah!

If only people knew my tortured thoughts. For many years I had been in control, or at least thought I was, and I was content to a point. But now I could fool myself no longer. Where did all this come from? Why was I feeling so adrift, so empty when I had so much? At that point in my life, I had no answer. It was many years later that it was revealed to me what had happened. The story of my experiences and what I learned and how my questions were answered has been an exciting one for me, and this is what I want to share with you. Perhaps it will be an encouragement for some who read this. I pray that it will. So back to one of my questions—who could possibly understand what I was feeling?

After a year or so of not attending church and my husband begging me to go to any church—just go—and my feelings of discontent not changing, I figured I had to do something. For reasons I could not explain at the moment, I felt led to call the retired minister of the Presbyterian Church I had attended for so many years because I trusted him. The minister, Dr. Hassebrock, invited me to his home. As I drove over, I kept thinking, *This is crazy. What answer can he have?* But I was at the breaking point. I simply could not go on like this any longer. I had so much; but I had nothing.

His living room was warm and inviting. His wife sat quietly by me, a calming influence.

I poured out my story. I cried buckets of tears. From the depths of my heart I asked him, "What is wrong with me?" "Why am I thinking these things?" He took my hand, and with gentleness told me nothing was wrong with me that couldn't be fixed. "God" he said, "is growing you."

Growing me? What did he mean? Then Dr. Hassebrock told me there was nothing wrong with the church I was attending, but I needed to find a place where I could grow in an understanding of God's plan for me. I must start visiting churches. The name over the door didn't matter, just as long as it preached the truth of Jesus. He promised I would know when the right church was found. He believed God was calling me into special service for Him. He prayed with me and said he felt honored to be part of God's calling one of His own. To say I was perplexed is an understatement. I certainly had not expected this kind of consolation or encouragement. He prayed with me. He expressed confidence that things would be better, but said I needed to begin searching in order to understand the calling God had on my life.

I really didn't understand any of this. I thanked Dr. Hassebrock and his wife for listening and giving me guidance. I sat in my car, tears still streaming down my face. I kept thinking of the statement Dr. Hassebrock had made, "God is growing you." Then I thought about the other statements he made, to go to a church that preached the truth of Jesus and God was calling me into service for Him. What did these things mean? All of a sudden I felt a calmness, a determination coming over me. I remember saying aloud, "Okay, God, I'll visit some churches. I'll search for something, but I'm not sure what it is I'm searching for." (As I share this with you now, I wonder, if I hadn't deep-down believed in God, would I have been searching?)

Actually, I was a little scared, overwhelmed by what I had been told. If I followed this challenge where was it going to take me? But the alternative was an emptiness of which I was so sick and tired. There had been enough of that in my life lately. Also, the idea that there was a plan for my life stirred a longing deep inside me to count for something more than what I saw on the surface of living day by day. Having goals and striving to accomplish them has always been a challenge and delight for me. Little did I know that day was to be a turning point in my life. Nor could I have possibly imagined how the prophesy of those four words the minister spoke, "God is growing you" would start a chain of events that continues to bring me such peace and such joy every day of my life.

Fear of Stepping into the Unknown

I do not think it is ever easy to step into uncharted waters. When we are plodding along in our comfort zones, we believe we are safe or secure, or at least treading water. Stepping into the unknown, or beyond the comfort zone, is an act of faith. This faith for the ordinary person is faith in himself or herself. For a Christian, this faith is trusting God will help, and believe me, at that time, my faith was really small in trusting God. Apparently God was showing me that the quality of my life was shallow. I had used up all my own ideas, and they weren't working. What caused me to finally turn to God? Desperation for one thing, and fear for another. Although at the moment I couldn't grasp it, God was giving me another chance to walk with Him, to know Jesus in a way beyond my understanding at that time.

However, at that moment, I simply sat there in my car going over all that had transpired and thinking, *What in the world is happening to me?* I went home, went on with my daily life, but periodically I mulled over the minister's comments. After a few weeks I decided to see if there would be help for me in visiting some churches. I visited churches sporadically. I didn't find the right church overnight. But always there was this feeling—this drive—to keep looking. One Sunday I visited a church not too far from home. The people were friendly. I listened intently to the message the minister gave. I was drawn back again and again. My husband was happy to see me going back to church. At this point, nothing Dr. Hassebrock told me had happened except I started looking into who I was. I was beginning to step into those uncharted waters.

What if I had said no way to that minister's suggestions and had instead decided to deal with it somehow in my own strength thinking I could get through it? What if I had turned my back on the experience of knowing Jesus? When we put up barriers or invisible walls around our emotions—our feelings—not only do we shut out people, we also shut out God. I had good walls built up. No one could get closer than I allowed. But I allowed just enough that most people thought I was friendly, fun, worldly enough to accept off-color jokes. I enjoyed parties, ignored racist remarks, figured things that I didn't approve of simply were not my business. So my walls were pasted over with attitudes of indifference, lack of compassion, understanding of where others were coming from, definitely a don't-get-involved type awareness, a not-my-problem attitude (except when it came to my children or my husband). Sound familiar?

I believed—I had to believe—that basically I was a good person, and my decisions were right. How else could I survive the loneliness of rejection that was always under the surface? Now my life was good. In fact, on the surface I believed I was truly happy. I laughed a lot. People have often commented about what a smiling person I am—even before this hunger for something more started driving me into a search. There was nothing wrong with my husband, my children, my mother, brother, or any other family member. It was simply something inside me. Now if I could not blame any family member for my problem, who was left? Just me! Think that didn't shake me up? Here was this confident, self-assured woman realizing for the first time she was not perfect, not in complete control, not able to slough off the feelings of panic, the fear of forever, or the fear of dying.

Finally, I was back in church again. The year was 1981. Only this time something was very different. The people in this church wouldn't let me slip in and out. And at least I stayed to shake hands with the minister, which, of course, gave people the opportunity to speak to me. Perhaps inside I was being pulled to become more friendly, just a little more open. I don't know, and I don't have the answer. But I do know this was something new for me. The minister, Rev. J. Michael Mullin, was welcoming. He made me feel at ease. I remember one time Pastor Mike came to my home to visit. We talked about my beliefs. The issue of the apostle Paul came up. In my usual know-it-all attitude, I said that Paul was a chauvinist and that I didn't agree with what he said. The pastor just smiled and went on talking. Now you have to realize that I had never actually read all of Paul's letters in the Bible. Another one of my preconceived ideas. As time went by, some of the people at the church invited me to join an adult Bible study. *Why not?* I thought. If I was to learn more about this God I had questioned, perhaps a class would be a good way to learn.

I have never been one to keep my mouth shut. If I have an opinion, it will usually surface. If I have a question, out it comes. This class was no different. Much of what I heard was acceptable, but there were some issues with which I disagreed. In one of our discussions I was referring to God in some grand way. One of the men in the class asked me, "Evelyn, why don't you ever mention Jesus?" I said, "Jesus and God are one and the same, aren't they? What's the difference which name I use?" The man very kindly didn't pursue it.

I didn't know there was a difference at that point, but the question stayed with me. Every so often the question would pop into my mind. I started listening more carefully to what the minister said during his sermons and his prayers. I noticed that many of the people referred to Jesus as someone they knew. How could this be?

The Growing in God

This searching and growing has taken much time, so as I try my best to explain how it happened to me, please keep in mind it was not just a one day or one month growing, but a growing that just seemed to happen gradually over a long period of time. While this growing was starting, I doubt anyone noticed any difference in me. But did I ever begin to notice a difference! For one thing, I was getting to know more people in this small church than I had in twenty-five years at the previous, big church. It did not seem to make any difference that I came alone anymore. In the past, my excuse had been that my husband was not with me, therefore I wasn't part of the group. Funny how we make excuses to cover our own inadequacies, our insecurity, or our need to keep that wall in place.

I remember one Sunday in class I made one of my sweeping comments. Yes, at that point I was still doing that. There was a woman sitting by me. A look crossed her face that said to me, "You are being too critical, too all-knowing, and you are wrong." She did not speak to me, but just got up and left in a hurry. Instead of my usual, it-doesn't-bother-me attitude, I questioned myself. *What did I say? How did I say it? What kind of impression am I making? Who is that woman, and what kind of Christian is she?*

Do you realize what was happening to me? I was allowing a chink in that wall I had built up around me. I was saying I care about what people think rather than not caring. Have you been there? It is hard, isn't it, to let down the guard. Who knows what kind of feelings will emerge? At this point I did not have a personal relationship with Jesus, nor did I understand the ministry of the Holy Spirit, but I had reached the point where I could truly say I believed there was a God, who was God the Father, Jesus the son, and the Holy Spirit, all in one God. Did I ever have a lot of learning to do! The Holy Spirit must have thought, "What a challenge we are facing with this woman!"

During this time my oldest daughter Camille, married and living in Texas, more than a thousand miles from me, was drawn into this searching I was doing. We talked, and I questioned her about her newfound faith in the Episcopal denomination. She came home for a week's visit, and I just fired questions at her, one after another. Years later she told me, "Mom, I was scared that I couldn't answer, and you were so determined to get answers. I just kept praying for the Holy Spirit to help me." Her answers gave me more things to think about. I saw her husband, Jon, reading the Bible. He is very intelligent, a professor in economics, so I figured if he had questioned and apparently found enough satisfactory answers to join a church with Camille, then I needed to do more searching.

Covered in Prayer

Camille belonged to a prayer group in her church, although I did not find out until years later that for two years those women faithfully prayed for me. They prayed that I would find Jesus, that I would be touched in a special way, that I would open my heart to the Holy Spirit, and God heard these dear, faithful women's prayers. These women did not know me. My daughter simply described my situation and asked if they would pray with her during the weekly prayer time together. They were faithful. Camille kept them informed of my progress, my discouragement, my anger, resentment, and through all of this, I did not dream there were people a thousand miles away caring enough about me to lift my situation up to the Lord. Now we know God is the instigator of prayer, so that means God was calling to his faithful prayer warriors to pray for a woman He wanted to bring into His kingdom. That also has shown me that in my crying out, my saying "Are you really God? Do you really care?" He heard! He responded! He loved me that much—in spite of my doubt, my turning away from Him.

A thought from the present: I hope, dear reader, you too respond to God's call at any time to pray for others. We all need to be covered in prayer, and we never know what barriers are being torn down in the spiritual realm between our God and the person for whom we are praying. Sometimes we won't ever hear about the success of how God answered the prayers, yet God calls us to be faithful in expectation that He will answer. At times we might be given a glimpse or even a testimony of how God answers our prayers. When this happens, I believe this is one of God's ways of rewarding our faithfulness.

Not long after I had made a personal commitment to Jesus Christ, Camille told me about the two-year prayer commitment of these women. I was amazed and overwhelmed. To think of their faithfulness for so long to pray for me and the power that is released through the prayers of these precious women just rocked me. Camille said they all rejoiced in my newfound belief in Jesus Christ. Not long after she shared this with me, I visited Camille in Texas. While there, I was invited to attend the prayer meeting of these women who had prayed for me for so long. What a joy that time was. I was able to witness what the Lord had done for me and how His Holy Spirit was teaching me the power of prayer and filling me with such joy. I had the opportunity to thank each of them for their dedication and perseverance in praying for me, and then I had a chance to pray with each of them.

Let me say right here, this was such a humbling experience. I felt so completely unworthy of their dedication in praying for me and yet so very thankful they had persevered. Would I have found Jesus without their constant years of prayer? Perhaps not, or perhaps it would have taken much longer. I just know it was a gift of love from a group of women that I will treasure all my life.

Witnessing a Miracle

During the first four years of my searching, I struggled to find answers to my many questions. God was definitely creating changes in my life. I found myself eager for each new experience. Although my mother was a member of the Lutheran denomination, she enjoyed hearing our pastor and often came with me.

At one service it was mentioned there was going to be an evening service with guest speakers, Bill and Delores Winder, from Fellowship Foundation. The Winders have a healing ministry.

I turned to Mother after the service and asked her if she would like to attend that event. Mother had macular degeneration. She could not drive a car, see to write or read, or see colors. Her response was a big yes. When the evening arrived, I must tell you, again I was facing a new experience. For one thing, I did not believe in physical healings. I thought these were all fake setups. I understood nothing about the miracles of healing that are based on scripture. But I knew mother believed in healing services and I thought, *Why not?*

God had other plans for me that night.

The sanctuary was filled with people. There was a time of praise and worship with lovely songs. Then Delores Winder spoke about her own healing and how it affected her life. She had written a book, *Jesus Set Me Free,* that describes her healing in detail. Finally, she asked for people to come forward for healing prayers. Though we were fairly far back in the sanctuary, Mother jumped up and said, "I want prayer." She went forward. Do you think I went with her? No, I just sat there as in a daze. But I could hear every word Delores was saying to mother. I could hear Mother's responses. I don't know how I heard since I was at least half-way back in the church, but I did. Different feelings were being evidenced. I felt as though I was there but not there. I felt a tingling all over and felt as if I weighed nothing. I was aware of these feelings but not afraid or not even questioning. The moment was beyond my control. Sounds seemed to echo in my head. Mother came walking toward me, and I got up to help her. She put her hands over her eyes and said, "My eyes feel like they are pulling. Oh, they feel so strange." We sat there for a few minutes and then Mother said "I believe I am healed, but should I ask Delores about continuing the eye drops?" My response, "No, Mother, let's just go home." At this point I felt I was simply on auto pilot. I picked up a little booklet regarding what to do after a healing. I tucked it in my purse.

Now here is the astounding part of the story. When we got to Mother's apartment, we talked about the experience. She said, "I really think I can see better." I asked her, "Mother, what color is the blouse I have on?" "Why Evelyn, it is brown with green leaves and peach-colored flowers." And I said, "How can you know that Mother, since you can't see colors?" She jumped up and ran to the bathroom door, saying, "Oh, I want to see the color of my new bathroom rug." She turned on the light and exclaimed, "It is a beautiful raspberry color." For the next ten years mother could read very large print, write her own checks, see colors, and was totally independent except for driving. I took her to the eye surgeon a few days after the healing had taken place. His comment, "With the scar tissue she has, there is no way she should be able to see as she does. I cannot tell you why this has happened, but I do believe in miracles."

How was I reacting to all of this? At Mother's house that first evening, I read some of the booklet to her that emphasized how it was important for her to deny any doubts Satan might try to put in her path because he always wants to take away anything that will bring us into a closer relationship with Jesus. We prayed together. Mom said, "I will tell Satan to go away if my eyes start getting cloudy." I agreed, yet was not sure what all this meant. Was I astounded? Was I questioning? Was I impressed? All I can tell you is that I was a changed woman from that night forward. As I look back on that time, I believe the Lord just zapped me big-time with an overflowing of the Holy Spirit. Interestingly, I only see this as I look back. At the time, I was just floating along with whatever seemed to be happening. I particularly remember feeling a sense of peace, of everything being all right, a don't-sweat-it kind of feeling. To this day my mother says she believes Jesus healed her to bring me into a special relationship with Jesus and the Holy Spirit. She might be right; moms often are.

Right after this happened, I began desiring to learn more about how to study the Bible and how to understand scriptures that seemed very deep and unexplainable. I started reading Christian books by authors with sound biblical teaching, especially ones about the Holy Spirit and about the healing ministry of Jesus Christ. I often asked Pastor Mike whether a specific book would be helpful or if it was based on truth. As I began to open up and ask questions of people at church, friendships began to form. These friendships were different than any I had experienced in all of my life up to that time. Jesus was referred to often. Words of praise and thankfulness were always floating around. And I began to pray. Oh, what stilted phrasing I used! My needs, my desires, my wants were listed day after day. But I was at least speaking to God, believing He must be listening. That was a big, big step for me. Remember the woman I mentioned in the Sunday school class who gave me the look that started me questioning my attitudes and beliefs? Her name was Bettilee Perkins, and over the years, she has become a very close friend.

CHAPTER 2

The Journey of Growing

Dear reader, I now want to take you on the journey of my experiences with learning about the Lord. I'll share my joys, my mistakes, what I have learned about the power of prayer, about listening to God, His wonderful ways of rewarding my obedience, the joy in learning how to look for His signs and wonders.

In 1986, I started to journal many of my thoughts, experiences, and questions, and have been journaling ever since. Of course, I never dreamed the Lord was going to encourage me to write a book when I started. Where would I have been without all these journal entries to refresh my memory? It has taken eleven years for me to reach the point where I feel I can begin to express in writing the joy the Lord has given me in obedience to His call. I am still learning each day. I believe that I will always be learning—even unto death to this life. But what a wonderful, exciting walk I have been having with Jesus, not only my Savior and Lord, but my friend. I often picture Jesus sitting by the Father, interceding again for Evelyn. What a comfort to know He loves me so. If you don't believe Jesus loves you just as much, I hope you will continue to read this account of how I came to realize

His love for me, just one of His children. I pray it will help to stimulate your desire to have Jesus as your friend, your Savior, and your Lord. It has added such joy and serenity to everyday happenings. It has taken away fears. It has released abilities in me that I never knew were there. It has created friendships I cherish. It has shown me God's power in mighty ways. Above all, it has proven to me—God is! He is able to do all things.

Throughout the book I will do my best to explain some of the Christian jargon I came across and didn't understand. I've never read a book that has explained these things clearly to me, so I hope my explanations will be helpful to you. There are many books available that go in depth regarding a specific area of my experiences. If a particular topic increases your hunger to know more, I suggest you visit your local Christian book store. It might start a wonderful adventure in your life.

Our Prayer Closets

In Matt. 6:6 Jesus tells us to pray in secret and our Father will hear us. I have often heard that secret place referred to as a prayer closet. There was a time when I thought it meant I should only pray in a room with the door shut. I thought people who prayed together in groups were different, beyond my understanding. So what does this verse really mean? I believe there is a time when we need to pray privately, when we need to be alone with the Lord. When we are new in praying, being alone gives us freedom to say something without fear of criticism or of making a mistake in pronouncing our words or repeating a phrase, etc. Most people feel they are inadequate to pray aloud when they hear experienced prayer warriors belting out beautiful flowing prayers. When we are in the prayer closet, taking time to be with God, that surely pleases Him. We are being humble before God. There are times when we need to pray alone. We should never pray to impress others with our gift of prayer.

Before we can step out in a group-type praying time, which I talk about later and is wonderful, we need to understand the importance of prayer and why Scripture encourages us to pray so much. We need to give the Holy Spirit opportunity to build our confidence in ways to pray. What wisdom Jesus had in telling us to pray in secret. For prayer is not something to boast about. It is a calling to put the concerns of others above our own concerns. It is something we do because we love our Lord, are thankful to be His children, and want so much to serve Him, to praise Him, to honor Him.

The prayer closet should be a place where we can pray without others hearing us or disturbing us. It does not have to be a closet. I have prayed as I walk, when I was taking a bath, driving the car, gardening, washing the car, cleaning the house. What better way to make the mundane seem special? Any place where you can focus on the Lord is an okay place. As your prayer life grows, you will no doubt find yourself drawn to one specific place over and over to really communicate with the Lord. My favorite place is sitting on the floor in our family room early in the morning. I can look out the window and see trees, birds, sky, and feel the warmth of the sun as it comes through the window. When I feel called to get answers or direction for a decision, I usually end up there, my own little special prayer closet reserved for glorious times of prayer and comfort.

Remember my referring to a group of women praying for me all through my time of struggle? If Camille had told me at the beginning of my search that a group of women were praying for me, I would have had a flippant remark to make. I would not have been impressed, perhaps even irritated, thinking, *Who are they to pray for me?* I might have put additional barriers up, making it even harder for the Lord to reach me. My daughter was being obedient to Scripture, keeping the prayers secret for all that time, only sharing when she knew I could accept, and most importantly, when I was at the place where I could see the results of faithful prayer and that God truly answers the prayers of His dedicated and obedient people.

Symbols / Memories

Do you have one very special family member in your life? My grandmother was that special person for me. As a little girl, most of my memories are being with her as she and Grandfather raised me until I was eight years old. Mother had to work since my father had left us when I was only a baby. Grams, as I called her, was so wise. She never lectured or really scolded, but would tell a story and the example would hit home. She believed in me. That alone was a wonderful gift. She taught me how to sew, to love poetry, to enjoy watching nature, to see beauty in little things. All my life she has been my idol. I always thought if I could be just half the woman Grams was, I would be a good person. Grams studied her Bible and made notes about her thoughts most of her life, I guess. After her death, Mom gave me Grams' Bible and notebook. She certainly loved Jesus.

Many years ago, when I was just twenty-eight years old and she was eighty-eight, we went to a nursery to pick out a tree for my new home. We spent quite a while searching for just the right tree. It had to be a very specific kind of tree, Grams said, one that would grow tall, be strong, give lots of shade, and be disease resistant. She finally picked an English hard maple. After my husband planted it, Grams and I were admiring this four-foot sapling, and she put her hand on the little thin trunk and told me, "Evelyn, long after I am gone, this tree will be here to shade you and stand watch over your house. It can always be a reminder of how I feel about you."

As years went by, the tree grew and put forth new branches. Each fall I measured my sons' growth with the tree. It was not a fast-growing tree. At first it seemed as if my sons were growing faster than the tree. Whenever Grams came to visit we inspected the tree. Seven years later Grams died, and somehow I still recall her face and things she said to me when I was by that tree. My six children were all aware this was a special tree. They never carved on it or tried to break its branches. When the tree was twenty years old we decided to add a large room to our home to hold all our adult children and grandchildren when we had large gatherings. There was a limit to the room size because I stressed that the tree stayed. Even the workmen were careful with the tree.

And now, many years later, this great big tree shades the room and hovers over our deck. It has a twin fork in the trunk and is shaped beautifully. What I have noticed many times is this. The tree puts forth a feeling of the Lord. Birds build nests in it and sit on its branches and sing their beautiful songs. The wind rustles the leaves, and this creates a special sound of nature's music. Many times, when I feel uneasy, I can sit by this tree and listen to its song and I can recall Grams' words of wisdom (she had so many). This has become a great place to have conversations with Jesus (in warm weather) and always, always I leave with a sense of peace and fulfillment, knowing that God cares. He loves me and will see me through the current problem.

I believe this is one of the wonderful blessings God gives us when a loved one dies. He helps to heal our loss and then continually gives us wonderful memories that we can recall with joy and a sense of peace. It soothes the missing of the loved one and brings gentle smiles to our faces. Tears are those of happy times and a thankfulness this person was in our life, no matter for how long or for how short a time. I never thought when we were buying a simple little tree for the yard that someday it would help me recall the love of a very special woman. I never dreamed that I would be sitting in the shade of that tree and having a conversation with Jesus. I believe, however, my grandmother knew this would come to pass. Little things. Ordinary things. They can have such an impact on our lives. How often do you think the Lord encourages each of us to create the spark with someone that will carry over into his or her life for many years to come? Our giving of time, listening to loved ones, sharing our love of Jesus, extending words of encouragement, letting the person know we believe in him or her are all little things. Yet they can become the link to a person's ability to have wonderful self-esteem. Our giving of whatever it might have been will possibly be just what the person will recall at a specific time to seek a relationship with Jesus. Grandmother gave me such a gift. I pray to pass it on.

Healing Prayer

I want to tell you about an experience I had in December 1985. This was one of the first times I really sought the Lord for a healing. Yes, my attitude about healing had definitely made a turn-around after mother's eyes were touched. I had gone to the doctor because of pain in my lower spine at the tailbone. He was very concerned and ordered X-rays. I asked him what it could be, and his answer made me fear it was cancer. I talked to Pastor Mike of my church about it and asked for prayer and prayed many times myself.

On the way home from a Sunday night prayer service I felt such an urgency to talk to the Lord. I was alone in the car, so out it poured—aloud. I told the Lord how frightened I was and not ready to leave the world yet, but if He had decided it was my time, I would accept, but please give me a sign. I was crying so hard I could hardly see to drive. Good thing it was a back road. A quick vision of myself as an old lady passed before me. There were people around me, and I looked content. I was not allowed to see the faces of the others, but I knew it was me. I immediately knew that my time was not yet and the Lord had more work for me to do. Peace flowed through me and I thanked Jesus and the Holy Spirit for being with me and letting me have that insight. Later, when the doctor talked to me, his first comment was, "You do not have cancer," so he was also concerned, just as I had thought. The pain eventually went away without any treatment. This was a very important lesson for me in learning to lean on God, of giving over my control, of trusting Him.

And from this experience I learned that Jesus truly is the Great Healer. From my vantage point nineteen years later, I can say with assurance the Lord heals today just the same as He did two thousand years ago. Jesus is our Healer, and by His name our prayers are answered, but not always in the way we ask. He does it in ways that require our cooperation and our decision to accept the opportunities that God presents. God often puts an opportunity before us but we have to pray to be sensitive and aware of the signs. This is the work of the Holy Spirit in us. By ourselves we would not see or sense the working of God in situations around us. But through our prayers we become closer to God, and this allows the Holy Spirit to speak to us through situations, other people, and God's Word. I have come to understand that whatever problem comes up—and they will come— if I trust our Lord enough, if I pray for his will—his way and not my own—the solutions for the problems will be shown to me.

Our Lord has promised to never leave us or forsake us. He does not promise to always take away our problems, but He will give us the strength to bear them and help us to work through them. Is that not an awesome God? And what a huge growing step for me to accept this great Good News.

I am beginning to learn to believe God; to believe He is truly able to do all things. This has taken me a long time. There have been plenty of trials, mistakes, hesitancy on my part to reach out for this along the way, but just as His Word says, God is faithful (Lam. 3:22-23). He waits, always ready to give when we ask according to what His will is for us. When Jesus left us to be with the Father, He did not leave us unprepared to fight the enemy. We have the Holy Spirit sealed within us (2 Corin. 1:22). We have God's Word always available. We have the fellowship of other Christians in the church family. We have the ability to come into the presence of the living God in our prayers and speak directly to Him. We have the gift of salvation in Christ Jesus by the grace of the almighty God. We can confess our sins and choose to repent (to turn away from the sin) thereby establishing a closer relationship to Jesus. We have such hope.

Do you believe Jesus can heal? Do you believe He will heal your pain? Do you believe His healing is only for others? Believe me, Jesus loves you just as much as He loves me. If He will heal my pain, He will heal yours. What is the secret? Surrender—the surrender of self, and this is no easy thing. The world has taught us to be independent. We are capable. We can do anything if we persevere or know the right person or do the right thing. But this is not what God calls us to do. We are to lean on Him. The more we surrender our control the more He will work in us, and remember, I was a woman always in control (or so I thought). This revelation of leaning on God began to set me free.

While we are waiting for answers to prayer, whether they are for physical healing or situational concerns, we must continually give the Father praise, honor, adoration, and thankfulness. Our act of faith in believing that God is able is a very important part of our prayers. We must remember to be patient because our God sees the overall picture of a given situation, not just the tiny part we can see. He knows what is truly best. We don't need to give Him a "how to" list. After all, He is the all-knowing God. We must let Him know we believe He is able, that we surrender our needs to Him, that He has all the answers, the "master plan." It is pleasing to our Father for us to acknowledge to Him how very mighty and wonderful He is, even if He isn't answering our prayers the way we want or as quickly as we want. Are you starting to get the picture?

God could do all this without us. He does not need our prayers to solve problems, to heal sickness, to create opportunities, to change lives. But our God loves us so much that He wants us to want to come to Him, to seek His help, to trust in Him. Our Heavenly Father has so much love for us. He desires us to turn to Him for comfort, guidance, assurance, strength, forgiveness, and understanding. These are just a few of the many gifts He has for each of us. I did not understand it twenty-some years ago, but what a joy to begin learning this and accepting God's truth from His Holy Word, the Bible. It doesn't matter who we are, what our lifestyle is, whether we are rich or poor, whether we are worldly successes. It only matters that we are willing to surrender our control and seek the help of the Lord.

I want to share another example of how our surrender to God's will works in healing. During 1986, while still working, I started occasionally having blurred vision. The page of the document I was working on would fade and things around me would have double lines or jiggle. My head ached. If I closed my eyes for a few minutes it went away. I said nothing, ignoring the possibility of anything serious. Then, in October of that year while at Sunday worship, I heard in my spirit, the words, "Be fearful, praise, not criticize." In my mind I retorted, *Fearful of God?* and the answer came back "No, fearful of Satan." The only reason I remember this is because I had written it in my journal. At that moment, I had no idea what this meant. I was beginning to accept the fact that I should listen, record the thought, and trust. For me, this was a step-at-a-time kind of acceptance. Some days I did it without question, but on other days I really hesitated. And I just knew these were words I should not share with others.

I believe God will cover me with His protection each day, but I decided to watch for temptation. However, the words kept popping back into my mind periodically. Finally, one morning

I was awakened in the early hours with the words ringing in my mind, "Be fearful."

I thought whatever is brewing must be close at hand. I prayed the Spirit would help me be continually alert so I would know when this attack came. It frightened me. Satan is powerful, but not nearly as powerful as God. We must remember always that God allows Satan to be the temporary ruler of the world and therefore able to put temptation before us. It is all part of the terrible freedom of choice that the Lord has given us as a gift, which we have misused.

Later that morning, as I was preparing to take my youngest daughter Julia to high school before I went to work, I asked her, "Do you pray for others?" She said yes, so I gave her my journal to read what I have just described. She didn't say much, but as we got into the car she said, "Mom, do you know this song?" She sang these words: "Do not be afraid, I walk before you always. Just follow me and I will give you rest."

I dropped her off at school, dashed back home, and called my daughter Camille in Texas. I explained my concerns and asked for her prayers. As you can tell, I did not have all the answers myself and seeking the advice and wisdom of others was part of the new pattern of living I was learning. This was a big, big step for me. She said in her opinion God was getting ready to take me a giant step forward in my relationship with Him, and Satan was furious. She suggested I pray to bind Satan in the name of Jesus. So I did it right away.

Just to cover all bases, as soon as I got to work I called Pastor Mike and asked for his prayers. He prayed a beautiful prayer of protection over me. He told me I should be wary but not fret over the warning. It could be a good thing was going to happen and this caused Satan to be angry. Have you noticed how I was continually reaching out for wisdom and help and prayer from others? In other words, I was venturing out into trusting more in God and less in myself.

Around lunchtime my eyes started the blurring and loss of peripheral vision. I went to my car to rest my eyes. As I put up the front seat to climb in the back and stretch out, there lay on the floor a big blue button with printing on it, DEVIL POWER. It was one of the buttons kids collected representing the football team at my daughter's high school.

I just laughed and hid it under the mat. I prayed for release from the vision problem, relaxed, and in about five minutes all the symptoms went away. That night I told the pastor about what happened. He said a detached retina could cause this problem and suggested I contact a specialist to be sure nothing was wrong

I want to explain that even in the newness of my relationship with Jesus, I immediately started praying. I asked Him to take away any fear of blindness. I asked Him to give me a strong measure of trust and courage to contact a doctor right away. I deeply believed Jesus would help me with this burden of fear. The first week of November the eye specialist informed me that I was experiencing an optic migraine attack. Satan would have me afraid and trembling but with Jesus to pray to and to protect me, He conquers all. This was eighteen years ago, and I have not had a recurrence of this problem since. There was no treatment. The problem left just as quickly as it came. I also want to share with you that on November 5, 1986, I wrote in my journal the following: *Funny, but whatever was going to happen, Jesus protected me. The "be fearful" factor is gone, so this was the crucial day. I believe if I had not called on Jesus something bad would have happened. For some reason I feel sometime in my life I will write for others, to share the power of God, to reach the lonely, the confused, the troubled, the doubters and help bring them to a knowledge of the wonder of a relationship with Jesus.*

How did I know eleven years earlier that in 1997 God—by the power of His Spirit—would direct me to start writing a book? Little things that happen and often seem irrelevant, when put together over a period of time, show the power of God at work in our lives. It shows how He directs our paths, encourages our choices, and if we trust in Him and follow His guidance, what joy He has in store for us. I had completely forgotten that journal entry in 1986 about writing a book.

I can tell you right now, I have no idea how this book will ever get printed, distributed, or published. But I know I must write it, and I trust God to show me in His time what the next step will be. Before the book is finished I might have more to tell you about this situation. I don't call it a problem, because I have truly come to believe God will do it. I just need to be obedient to whatever He tells me to do and remember to give Him all the glory and all the recognition for whatever comes from this writing. (In 2004 I finished the book, had a first edit, and applied for a copyright. More steps. Yet it took me until 2005 to get up the courage to have this book printed.)

Resentment / Forgiveness

We often hold on to resentment toward another person. We let it eat away at our memories. It stirs up anger in us and can cause bitterness that shows in our voices when we speak of that person or situation. A big resentment, at least for me, was the result of a feeling of hurt that I had against my stepfather. Why? Because I didn't think he loved me as I thought he should, or at least he didn't show his love the way I expected him to. This goes way back to when I was a little girl of five or six. At that time, my birth father did not live with mother and me, and I came to learn later no one knew where he was. My mother worked to take care of me, and we lived with my dear grandparents (the grandmother I mentioned earlier). I always pretended my dad was dead so other kids wouldn't think he just left me, which is what he really did. Little kids can be cruel. I well remember one day when I was six, a large group of kids circled around me and started singing, "You don't have a daddy" over and over. As I tried to get out of the circle they bounced me back from side to side. When I finally broke loose and ran in the house to Grandmother, I cried and cried, saying, "I do have a daddy, but he's dead." Grandmother put her arms around me and told me gently but firmly I must accept the truth. My father was alive but lived far away and chose not to visit us, and it was not because of anything I had done. As I think back, I am grateful for my grandmother's wisdom. That day made such an impact on me that I even now get a sinking feeling as I write about it.

Despite my father's absence, I had a wonderful childhood. I had three uncles, grandparents, and a mother who all loved me very much and thought I was special. But for me there was always that doubt; *what is wrong with me that my father doesn't want me?* Then, when I was eight, mother married again. Now I had a daddy, and he was so good to me and was such fun to be with. He was a great big man and sang beautifully. I loved doing things for him. When I was nine, I received a darling baby brother, Charlie, who has been a good friend to me all my adult life. Dad and I always got along well until I married and started having children. Then he seemed to become critical and out of patience at times with my children. I was very ill after the birth of my fourth child and almost died. Dad never came to the hospital to see me. The years passed, and Dad became chronically ill. Much of the paperwork settling everything for mother became my lot to do. I had to be the one to talk to him about signing over his car, power of attorney, etc. when the doctors told us he was dying. My brother couldn't do it. Mom couldn't do it. And then Mom would say such things as "You're so hard, Evelyn." Dad died when I was forty-seven. I missed him but didn't even cry at the funeral; I just held it all inside. Time passed, but the hurt was still there. My memories of him were clouded with resentment for what I thought he did not do as a father should have.

On a Sunday morning in 1986, I was sitting in church. Pastor Mike was preaching, and to this day I couldn't tell you what he was saying, but the words were reaching deep down inside of me. In my mind, I heard this voice so clearly saying, "Evelyn, you expected more from your father than he was able to give. Your father loved you as much as he could, and you are not letting him rest in peace." This just blew me away. I couldn't wait to get out of church and into my car to think about it. And, yes, it was true that Dad had always been there for me. He always encouraged me, bragged about me, hugged me, and called me his very special daughter. I had put him on a pedestal, and, of course, he was bound to fall off. Why do we do things like this? Why do we punish ourselves by holding onto things that continue to hurt us?

I found there is a wonderful answer in Jesus. He is the great healer. Even though I was very new in understanding the power of forgiveness, the Holy Spirit was showing me what freedom from hurt really is. After a few days of thinking about what had happened at church, I finally reached the point where I knew I must pray. So I went to my favorite spot, knelt down on the floor, and started praying. I called out for understanding asking God who had been wrong, Dad or me. I forgave Dad for the times he hurt my feelings. I asked forgiveness for not speaking out and letting him know I was hurt. I thanked God for giving me this special father all those years of growing up. And do you know what? All the hurt faded away. I shared this experience with my husband, Bill. I sat on his lap, poured out these feelings and cried. Yes, I could finally cry over my dad's death, allowing my grief to be expressed. Bill just held me and comforted me. What a blessed release. Now whenever I think of Dad, it is with a good feeling, a thankfulness, and contentment. I remember the laughs, the special talks we had. The sense of being protected that I felt in his presence. All the bad memories were gone as if they had not happened. And beyond all that new awareness of my relationship with Dad, I began to realize that I had a heavenly Father who loved me unconditionally, would never leave me, never give up on me, who watched over me every day of my life. What joy, what comfort I have received so many times in learning and experiencing this, that I am a child of God.

I have come to realize that when we hold onto hurts, resentment, anger, or unforgiveness toward someone who has died, it creates an atmosphere for bitterness and self-pity that becomes a prime focus in our lives. It spills over into all of our daily living, our decisions, and our reactions to others. We become the walking-wounded. I learned that we don't have to be that way. God has provided a way out. When we ask the Lord to take all the hurt and resentment away, when we ask for forgiveness, He is so good. He not only takes these things away, He gives us beautiful memories or reminders to replace the emptiness within us. I can never thank our Lord enough for His compassion to minister to my hurt and resentment in a way that allowed me to fully love my father again and to remember him with thankfulness and appreciation for the role he played in my developing into a confident, stable woman.

A question for you, dear reader: If we seek God's comfort in our grief, why does God remove the memories of hurts when someone we love dies? Do you think it is because our grief could not be borne? Would we become bitter and so wrapped up in our own pain that we could not minister to others or function properly in this world? I believe taking away the bitter memories or reminders is God's way of releasing us from these hurts and helping us deal with forgiveness and understanding and repentance so that we can build on our relationship to Jesus. In this way we can also help to minister to others who have been or are going through the same kind of situation. He is such a faithful God and is always willing to help us if we ask. And the blessing is that we are not condemned by God for our inward self-pity or for nursing our hurts. Instead, we are encouraged to give them to Jesus so that we can be ministered to by the Holy Spirit and live in that freedom that Jesus came to give us (Luke 4:18-19). Often, in my talking to Jesus, I have said, "Thank you, Jesus, for releasing me from hurtful memories and allowing me to fully love my earthly father again."

For me, the hurtful memories left immediately, but that may not always be the case. For some it may take many times of prayer, of surrendering the hurts, of giving them to Jesus—and not taking them back. If we continually hang onto those hurtful memories, we cannot move forward into the blessed freedom that I mentioned. We are actually in bondage to the spirit of resentment—or bitterness or anger—whatever the particular memory might be in each individual's situation. It's as if we are walking on the side of the road that is muddy. With each step we take, we feel our foot being sucked into the mud, grabbing hold. If we step out of the mud onto the firm smooth path, we feel light, and our walk becomes springy. That's exactly what the Lord does for us. Who wants to struggle forever through the mud of misery when we can be free to enjoy the wonders that our God has created for us?

Servant Leadership

All through 1986 I continued to be awed by the movement of the Holy Spirit in my life. I began to understand things that had been only words others spoke. For instance, the words "Servant Leadership." I heard those words many times from the leaders of the church. I knew about leadership—that was part of my personality—but what was the *servant* kind of leadership? It finally came to me that this kind of leadership meant I must be open to whatever the Holy Spirit guides me to do. I should put aside my own wants and desires and listen to the Spirit. I needed to search for answers to help me be a better vessel through which the Holy Spirit reaches out to others. Bible studies, prayer, worship, listening, and questioning those who had become mature believers in Christ; all these activities were preparing me for what the Lord had planned for me.

When we are in servant leadership, our actions are more likely to be observed by others. We become somewhat of a role model for how a Christian is to act. This is a heavy responsibility, and a very humbling responsibility. We need to be more careful in how we speak of others. We need to remember in many situations we are representing the church beyond the one to which we belong. But even more than that, we are to be encouragers for those who are seeking a relationship with Christ Jesus. In worldly leadership, a person is usually very dynamic, one who goes for the decision that will improve the company regardless of employees and what might happen to them. These leaders are usually catered to. People are careful how they express ideas in front of these leaders. People usually defer to the leaders' ideas.

But in servant leadership, the leaders should be open to hearing from the people. Their decisions should be based on what they believe is best for the majority of the congregation they are serving. The glory for ideas and projects is given to the Lord. Humility, respect for the needs of others, a listening attitude, and a vibrant prayer life are all part of the makeup of a servant leader. A basic part of servant leadership is actually serving others. Be part of committees, supporting activities of the church, encourage the people in the worship and service of God, be willing to be teachers of the Bible. Actually I have come to understand that servant leadership is based on the model of Jesus, who came to serve not to be served. And, of course, who does the servant leader ultimately report to? Our Lord.

Along with this attitude of service, a very necessary part of this attitude is giving up feelings of ownership. Over the years I have seen people do a wonderful job of serving and then when someone new comes in with fresh approaches, there is resentment or non-acceptance. Ownership should never be a part of our servant leadership.

CHAPTER 3

The Ministry Begins

In January 1985, Pastor Mike asked if I would chair a prayer ministry. My immediate thought was *That's a laugh.* I glanced around, thinking he must be talking to someone else, but I was the only one standing there. Me? I would not even pray aloud in a group. I questioned much of what the Bible said—especially in the letters of Paul. Yet I said yes. Right away my plan was to get things moving fast, make a bunch of changes, do a survey, etc. Words of wisdom were given to me by Camille and one of the leaders of our church. "Keep it simple," they both said.

So how should I proceed? I was a complete novice, blithely unaware of what was going to happen to me over the course of the next nineteen years. I often think what a sense of humor our Lord has. I was very new in understanding how to trust in the guidance of the Holy Spirit, very new at prayer, very new in my personal relationship with Jesus. The previous five years of learning, of continually changing my viewpoint about God, of experiencing a new kind of bonding with fellow Christians, of letting people get close to my personal feelings, of being open about my lack of knowledge and asking lots of questions, had only begun to prepare me for this new challenge.

As I have looked back over my journaling, I realize now how much Pastor Mike stretched me. He gave me opportunities to grow by requests such as the one I just mentioned. What a brave pastor he was. I know I made plenty of mistakes. There must have been times when he wished he had never asked me. The Lord clearly led me to the church that would give me a great opportunity to help God grow me.

Even in the new experience of starting a new ministry, I was ready to believe that the Holy Spirit would help me. I had reached a place where I trusted in Jesus enough to believe I could follow without fear. So began the transformation of Evelyn.

Keep in mind, at this time in my life I still had my husband and one daughter at home. I worked full time, was serving in leadership on the Session of our church—lots of commitments. At that time I did not think it necessary to set priorities on my commitments. I just plunged right in. First, I pulled together a prayer committee of three people. We organized a prayer meeting time on Sunday evenings. Usually about six to eight people attended. We had a time of teaching on Scripture (about five minutes), sang some worship songs, and then prayed. This was always an enjoyable time. There is a definite bonding between people when you meet on a regular basis and share prayer concerns, pray for one another, and worship together. I highly recommend these small prayer groups to be formed in every church.

Of course, this new area of my life was spilling over into my work life, even when I was not aware of it. I found myself praying for the Holy Spirit to give me confidence, to guide me, and to just be with me when I was making presentations or going into a big meeting. And God is so good. He always honored my request. Do you think it was because I was learning to lean on Him instead of on myself? (Prov. 3:5-6). Here is a little equation that is helpful to our relationships with other people.

HUMBLENESS+PRAYER-EGO=CONFIDENCE

You might find applying this to your life will give you freedom beyond anything you have ever experienced. Each time I remember to apply it to myself it really works.

I began to really understand who God is. Of course, this was just a beginning. I would get so excited about a new revelation that I wanted to share it with everyone, yet many times I needed to keep it to myself. Budding new Christians are so energized and so full of joy at receiving all these wonderful uplifting feelings that we tend to go overboard in expressing these feelings to others. A mature Christian understands this and encourages new Christians and loves them in all their exuberance. As I look back on this period of my life, I realize all the bubbly feelings and revelations being open to me were for building my need of Jesus Christ in my life. Here is one of the revelations that was meaningful for me at that time and that I entered in my journal.

God is forever.
His light is forever.
His power is beyond all measure.
His mercy falls on those who love Him.
So lift up your heart and your hands in praise of Him.
For He loves you so.

I want to share with you in this chapter some of the things I learned during my many years of being involved in the prayer ministry. Actually, throughout the book you will find me continually going back to prayer references and how different experiences brought me an additional understanding of how prayer affects our lives.

Receiving Words from the Lord

This is a delicate area for discussion. I want to share a little about what I have learned over the years—and continue to learn about sharing what I hear in my spirit. Many people recoil when you say to them, "The Lord told me…" I think this is because the person immediately feels you are stating a more personal relationship with the Lord then he or she has. I definitely believe the Lord is able to speak to all His children, but many do not take the time to listen, do not really want to hear, or do not believe God would speak to them. Perhaps it is better to say something like this, "In my spirit I sensed or heard …." This eliminates the superior attitude you might unknowingly present. The person can then either accept or not accept whatever you share. There are many times the Lord will speak to one's heart and it is not to be shared. I believe a great deal of the time this is true.

Usually when we hear from the Lord, it is not an audible voice. Sometimes it is in a confirmation received when another person affirms a thought you have received in your spirit. Sometimes it is a scripture that jumps out when you read it and speaks to what you are searching for. Sometimes it is a gut feeling. A feeling that just keeps returning and returning until you do not have any rest from it until you act upon it. So then what do we do with the words we hear in the deep recesses of our minds or in the intellect of our hearts? We can write the thoughts down in a journal. Read them over occasionally and, above all, pray to our Lord about what we have received.

For example, let's say we are praying for John's job situation. We sense that John is to take a new job. He must quit what he is doing and venture into a new area. Should we rush to tell John this? No. Then how do we handle an insight we think we have been given? We should be praying for John to have a listening heart, to be open to whatever the Lord might have planned for him, to be willing to accept the guidance of the Holy Spirit in whatever way God wants to change or not change an area in his life. We might want to pray God's blessings upon John. Our prayers can help in the heavenlies (the spiritual realms) to break down barriers that might be present for the Lord to reach John and do whatever it is that He desires.

Most of the time we will not know the end result of what was revealed to us. That does not matter. We must just be obedient to what the Lord is calling us to do at that moment, and most of the time it is *not telling* the person what he or she should do. This is a dangerous area to activate because we only see a fragment of the whole picture. Our advice, even when given in good faith, might be just the opposite of God's plan for that person.

In the example given above, you can see that the prayers were not giving God directions, nor was it a time to rush to the telephone and give John directions. It was a time to cover John with protection and an openness for him to receive what God desired for him.

However, there might be a time when you continually feel a need to share a particular insight with someone. If you have prayed and asked the Holy Spirit if this is right, and if you feel at peace about doing it, then may I suggest that when you approach the person, first ask him if he would like to hear what you felt in your spirit was a special word for him. If the person is ready to hear, he can say yes, and you can proceed. Remember to always give only the words you received. You do not need to embellish them or try to explain them. The words are meant for that person and if they are truly meant for that person, they will be accepted and understood regardless of whether you completely understand them. The words given are from a messenger, not a counselor.

What if the person says no when you tell the person you have received words in your spirit? You must be prepared to accept that with a gentle smile and a that's-all-right attitude. It does not necessarily mean the person disbelieves you or thinks you are interfering in his or her life. Probably the time is just not right for that person to receive. You have done what the Holy Spirit has led you to do—offer the opportunity to receive the words. Your job then is to simply pray however you feel led regarding the situation until you feel a release in your spirit. Understanding this and putting it into practice releases one from becoming a know-it-all in the eyes of others. It deepens our prayer life in that we are allowing God to control situations instead of thinking we have to do it. Joy is ours when we surrender our control over situations and allow God to do what He is really good at doing—running our lives.

A gentle reminder—often when we rush to share what has been released in our spirits we are allowing ego to control us. This makes us feel good. We are being a "do-gooder." This is not what we are called by God to be. We are to be examples of Christ-like love. Would Jesus rush to be a do-gooder? I doubt it. From the Scriptures it seems to me He always took situations to His Heavenly Father. He allowed people to choose. He never forced them to hear. He always stood firm in what He believed, that God was sovereign. Since Jesus is our role model, wouldn't this be a good pattern for us to follow? Here is the formula I suggest for this kind of situation.

Pray first
Ponder it
Ask for permission to share
Speak truth only
Do it in love
Give God all the glory.

Having stated the importance of being very careful in sharing messages we receive, I want to give a few instances where it seemed right and apparently helpful to the person for me to share.

In the fall of 1987 we were using prayer request cards at our church for people to express prayer needs. These were put in a box and then a member of the Prayer Ministry would take the card and pray over it during the following week. This one particular week I was praying over a request. I lifted the person to the Lord and then found myself praying for specific areas of her life that were not listed on the card. I said, "Wait a minute, Lord, why am I praying for these things?" Then I felt prompted to jot the thoughts down on the card. Throughout the day I kept thinking I must call this person and tell her what message I received. (Ponder it.) I argued with myself, since in the past I had experienced an unpleasant result in rushing to give a message to a person who was not ready to receive. The nudging, however, would not leave me. I asked the Lord to give me a peace or a sign about whether to share or not. (Pray about it.) Then I called this person. I explained that I had been given the prayer request card and found myself praying over areas not listed on the card. Did she want to hear what they were? (Ask for permission.) Since her answer was yes, I explained I did not need to know if any of these areas were a problem or how they applied to her life. But if they did, here was what I had been led to pray. (Speak truth in love.) After giving the message, she said to me, "Oh, Evelyn, could I have that card back with your notes? The message exactly touches on my problem." We then both shared our thoughts on how good our God is. (Give God the glory.)

That same fall I received a message during prayer time for my grown son Tom. Believe me, it is no easier to contact a family member than it is a friend or acquaintance. I waited five days, arguing with myself, *Yes, I'll call; no, I shouldn't.* Finally, since I didn't get a release from thinking about the message, I decided to just ask him if he wanted to hear it. He was open to hearing. We set a time, and I shared what I had heard. It did not mean a thing to me except it sounded like a warning. Tom seemed to know exactly what it was all about, thanked me for sharing, and told me any time I felt led to share anything with him to call.

So what did I do with this situation after sharing the words with Tom? Just one thing. I prayed to the Lord for protection around Tom every single day. I thanked Jesus that Tom belonged to Him and that Satan had no right to him as Tom was part of the family of God. To this day I know nothing more about that situation, and looking back I realize I don't need to know because God was and is in control. I noticed an interesting change regarding Tom's relationship with Jesus from that time on; Tom seemed to feel very comfortable with a sure knowledge that God was watching over him. Perhaps that was what the whole thing was about.

We must remember God uses us in many ways, and we are only one part of a much bigger plan that He has for His children. If we allow our ego to take over, we want the credit, we want to know all the facts of a situation, and we want to give advice. I don't believe this is how the Father wants to use us. It is His glory, His credit, and His plan. A good question to ask yourself when the old ego tries to take over is, *Do I really think I know better than God how to handle this situation? Do I think God doesn't always have all the answers?* Until we reach the point where we truly believe that only God has the true answers, we will be struggling daily with the old ego problem. I think most of us will always struggle with the problem because we are continually bombarded by all forms of media stating our ego is the way to go. We must constantly remind ourselves that we are in the world but not of the world. Jesus has made us overcomers of that which is evil and gives us awareness of situations that could pull us away from Him. Isn't that an uplifting thought? Doesn't that make your shoulders straighten with relief?

What about the opposite end of hearing from the Lord? What if someone comes to you and states that he or she has heard from the Lord regarding you? Years ago I was so impressed when someone said this to me. I listened and often wondered, *What should I do with this?* Now I know a little better how to handle or accept what a person might share. First, I take into consideration where the person is in his or her walk with the Lord. Secondly, I receive the message and thank the person. I jot down main points of the message. Third, in my quiet time with the Lord, I ask Him to give me guidance on whatever the message was about. Most importantly, I take no immediate action on the message until I have a chance to share it with the Lord, especially if there are a bunch of "you ought to" instructions in the message or there are parts of the message that are not builder-uppers.

If it is a negative message, I question it. A negative message is one that makes you feel unworthy, like giving up. The negative message might set goals far out of ordinary reach or ask you to deny being with other Christians or serving the Lord in any way. It is a message that tries to separate you from God instead of drawing you closer. The message should not make you feel sad. I believe any message from our Lord draws us closer to Him, not away from Him.

As I mentioned before, God certainly can speak to each of us Himself, but there are times when He uses other people. One time a message was given to me that has encouraged me in receiving God's love and has comforted me many times. The person did not know me personally, knew nothing much of my past or relationships with family. Therefore, when I received a message of God's love and encouragement spoken to another for me it became something to treasure. There was peace in my heart and no doubt of the source. It was uplifting, not negative. It happened about the time I had gone through all the new awareness of forgiveness and understanding about my dad.

The message said that God loves me, He is my daddy, and I can call him "Abba, Father." It said His love for me is eternal, and He will never reject me. This woman was a visitor from another church. She knew nothing about me and had just been introduced to me at a prayer meeting.

Another way you can be reassured upon receiving a message is to take it to someone you trust who is a committed Christian. It might be your pastor, it could be your prayer partner, or it could be a good friend who is a Christian. Above all, take it to the Lord in your prayer time before taking any action suggested in the message. One of the things I have found about words received in the Spirit or in our hearts is not to rush out and do whatever the message says. We are to use the common sense God has given us. We need to be sensitive to what is the right timing for any action. Again, be alert to nagging doubts as to whether the message is truly what the Lord is calling or guiding you to do.

Praying in Unusual Situations

By 1987 I had been involved with this church for about six years and the prayer ministry for two years. I had prayed with many different kinds of people, but believe me it was a constant learning experience. Even today, seventeen years later, I realize I am still learning. I imagine this will always be a learning experience, so please don't think because you have not been praying for a long time for others or because this is a new area for you, that others are better. Not true. They have just had more opportunity to become experienced in relating to unusual situations. In January of 1987 I experienced a time of praying for others that left me shaken and humbled beyond anything I had previously experienced. Two men from the downtown area came all the way out into the suburbs to our church seeking help. No doubt they were consciously looking for financial help, yet through talking to them and listening to them (this included our pastor and four church members), I heard a cry for more to life than what they presently had. These men were destitute, jobless, homeless, and without family. They appeared to be alcoholics. They described how they stayed warm in cold weather. They talked about the drop-in shelter and the dirt, noise, and fighting that went on in the shelter. You might wonder why they didn't get jobs. However, a person needs money to buy a newspaper, transportation to get to the interviews, a telephone or place to be reached, decent clothes to make a good appearance, references, etc. Because of the poor choices these men had made, they had none of these. How can hope be instilled? In this kind of circumstance wouldn't it be difficult to believe God really loves them?

I felt fear, confusion, and desperation emanating from them. Both confessed their belief in Jesus Christ and asked for help and guidance from Him. Yet I wondered just how open their hearts really were to following Christ in their daily lives or whether these were words just mouthed in order to get some money. We prayed with them, and the minister gave them bus money. But after I went home and thought about it some more, I was overwhelmed with grief and compassion for these men. They were weak, and the weakness feeds on itself. It became clear how little in my comfortable, middle-class life I knew of the stress, temptation, and misery of the lonely—the destitute. I thought about the fact that when I go to bed at night I have a clean, comfortable bed to snuggle in. I know in the morning I will awake to a warm house with good food to eat. I have a loving, caring family around me. I have goals and an exciting job waiting for me each day. I am rich beyond measure. I asked myself, *How can I relate to the misery of people like this? How can God expect me to know how to pray and answer their needs? What must they think when they see a gold cross at my throat and sparkling diamonds on my hand?*

Then I was reminded that God will give the answers. I do not have to know all the answers myself. I must just love them as they are, have compassion for their plight, and judge them not. This was just a glimpse into another part of life to assist me in the calling of the prayer ministry, and no doubt more experiences like this will happen. Still, what was I to do with the wrenching and helpless feelings that overpowered me?

I have learned that in praying for others it is important to remember that we are only the vessel through which the Holy Spirit ministers to the one receiving prayer. There is no glory in it for us, nor do we have to appear wise or all-knowing. Our compassion for the suffering of others, whether physical or spiritual, will help us to be empathetic. But the burden of their problems should always be placed at the foot of the cross. What do I mean by that?

Remember, Jesus came and took all our sins upon Himself. He encourages us to come to Him and give Him our burdens (Matt. 11:28-30). When we try to solve the problems of those who come to us for prayers or if we take on their burdens, it can place us in a position where we cannot be used by the Lord to minister. We will be weighed down with dejection, frustration, etc. I remember once I was involved in a healing service, and a person sitting in one of the pews asked me to come and sit with her. She shared a prayer need. As I looked at her, it seemed as if I was looking deep into her eyes, and way down deep there was nothing there but despair and hopelessness. As I lay in bed that night, I started thinking about the woman and the horrible despair I had seen. My head started aching, and I tossed and turned. Then I remembered the wise advice from a woman of prayer about giving the situation to the Lord. I got up and went into the family room, and I prayed. I lifted the woman up to Jesus and laid the problem at His feet. I remember so well telling the Lord I couldn't stand the pain. I wept for her and yet received a release from anxiety when I gave the problem to

Jesus. God doesn't call us to fix it. We are to bring situations to Him in our prayers and trust that He will fix it. Actually, when I started understanding that God would fix it and it was not my responsibility, it released my concern and fear that I would make the wrong suggestion or that I could not solve a specific situation. Another area where pride takes over is when we allow the worldly views to express themselves in our belief that we can do it, that we have all the answers, that we are really wise. And, of course, where do these thoughts come from? They come from our old enemy, Satan. But when we are serving the Lord and we seek His wisdom, then we will be exposed to the greater wisdom of God.

We are called to pray for others. We are called to be encouragers, and above all to express the belief—the faith—that Jesus is the great Healer. God cares about each one of us and everything in our lives. Hopefully, we will help pave the way for the ministering of the Holy Spirit to each person we touch in prayer. Sometimes when we pray for others, the idea that someone cares enough to spend a few minutes of his or her time bringing the situation before the Lord and listening to the person's concerns helps that person to be open to hearing what God wants to speak to his or her heart. Again, we are just the vessels, paving the way for God's miracles. I can never begin to imagine why God would want to use me in this way. It is humbling beyond words, yet I rejoice each time I pray with someone and see tears of remorse or tears of release or tears of joy streaming down his or her face. Then I know that the Spirit of God has touched that person in some very special way. Dear reader, God can use you just as He has used me. Each of us is so special to Him.

Leaning on the Lord

During 1988, it seemed the Lord was continually building my understanding of His ability to do for me what I had never been able to do for myself. The lesson of trusting God was being imprinted on my mind and in my heart. This is not an easy step for someone who always thought, *I can do it!* To acknowledge that there are areas where I must surrender control to God is very scary. Yet each time I ventured forth and said to myself, *Okay, I'll trust the Lord on this and see what happens,* He always came through. I must tell you that many times the end result was more diverse than I expected. Almost always, the situation was handled differently than I would have handled it on my own. Sometimes I couldn't see where all this was headed. The big difference was in my attitude. I simply began believing God was able. And when I acknowledged this and stood back and allowed God to do what He truly was able to do, it always worked. Here is a poem—actually a prayer that came to me back at that time—about trusting our Heavenly Father.

Dear Father:
 When I am lonely and by myself
 I trust You to be my companion.
 When I am tempted to sin
 I trust You to keep me from it.
 When I am depressed and anxious,
 I trust You to lift my spirits.
 When I am crushed by responsibility and over-whelmed
  by demands of people on my time,
 I trust You to give me poise and a sense of purpose.
 I trust You to make me still inside.
 When I forget You,
 I trust You will never forget me.
 When I forget others,
 I trust You will prompt me to think of them.

When You take something or someone from me
that I want to keep,
When You refuse to respond to my questions or
answer my too-selfish prayers,
I pray that I will trust You, even then.

Written 1994

Learning to trust is very difficult for us for so many reasons. Perhaps a childhood of rejection or a schoolroom of belittling or failure to hold a job or relationships that fail—all these kinds of situations create mistrust. So when we are told to trust in the Lord there is the immediate reaction, *Right, and be hurt again or have my hopes dashed again.* How can we learn to trust that God fulfills His promises? We must read God's Word and pray for understanding of what we read. And then we simply have to believe the truth of God's Word. What helps us hold on to believing these truths? We must ask the Holy Spirit to give us understanding beyond our own. Daily prayer is very important. Worshipping in a church, listening to beautiful Christian music, reading Christian books written by those who have walked through the trusting process are all ways to help build our ability to trust that Jesus knows our needs and that He is rooting for us. I particularly like the thought that Jesus is sitting by the Father and continually speaking for us (Rom. 8:34).

It comes back to a decision on our part to say, *I know I am not always right. I know I cannot make everything perfect.* When we acknowledge in our minds and hearts this is true—and it is true for every single person whether we want to admit it or not—then we are at a point where the Holy Spirit can start working on teaching us to trust in Jesus. This is an exciting adventure. Life will never be the same. Opportunities often present themselves for a testing of this trust, and when we allow the Lord to handle it, the burden and the anxiety leave. In their place there is such a feeling of thankfulness. Of course, there is concern, there is an awareness of the situation. Sometimes we are called to take action, but always there is the realization that God is in control, not us. What a freedom! What a release this gives! Over the years I often said to myself, *Why did I wait so long?*

I am not saying if we trust in Jesus we will not have any problems. Of course we will, for Scripture tells us there will be trials and tribulations in this world (John 16:33). Sometimes the troubles seem so great, so overwhelming, we wonder how we can make it. I have found when this happens we must take one day at a time, not thinking about tomorrow or next week, but just focusing on getting through this day. Often it is just getting through the next hour. But our God is a faithful God and if we believe, ask, and trust that our God will help, we will be able to get through the problem even if it has to be moment-by-moment. Many times the problem is not taken away, and we have to deal with it.

Sometimes the problem results from choices we have made, and we have to deal with the consequences of our choices. But always God is waiting for us to call on Him, and He will see us through. Why would God wait for us to call on Him if we are doing something that doesn't please Him? God loves us with an unconditional love, an everlasting love, and there is no condemnation in that love for the person. That doesn't mean God accepts the bad choices we make or overlooks an action contrary to His commandments, but Jesus paid the penalty for our disobedience to God's commands. And because Jesus was willing to lay down His life for each and every person—and that includes all who have lived and are living and those yet to be born—we are accepted by our Heavenly Father. Awesome isn't it? Can you imagine love from a mere person that comes even close to this kind of love? And it is ours to receive.

The first time I realized that God loved me in all my mistakes, all my prideful ways, all my poor choices, I felt like shouting from the housetops. I wanted to close the doors of the sanctuary of our church and say to all present, "You can't leave until you realize and accept all the love the Father has for each of you. There is freedom, joy, peace, excitement, eagerness, anticipation of life like nothing you have ever experienced before." I shared this feeling with Pastor Mike. He laughed and shook his head, commenting about the joy the Holy Spirit had poured into me. My greatest prayer is that all people will come to know the love of our Father for each of His children in a very deep way through a personal relationship with Jesus Christ.

I must be very honest in talking about trusting Jesus and tell you that not every day was a good day. There were struggles to surrender my old ways and my self confidence to that of the Holy Spirit. There were times I wanted to pray, but the demands of my husband and children and home and work took over. I had to learn to give myself a specific amount of time but not feel guilty if something came up that displaced that time occasionally. I found that when a crisis occurred that took away my personal time with the Lord, I simply needed to deny myself reading the newspaper, watching a TV program, hunkering down with a good book, etc., and give that time to the Lord. I found that making excuses not to give the Lord time each day was simply that—excuses. Even with a home and children there is time, perhaps it is only ten minutes, but the effort to concentrate totally on the Lord at some point each day is a must. I can't describe all it does for you, but by denying self we are surrendering our control to Jesus. We are putting Him first. We are expressing our love and awe. We are being obedient, and of course Scripture tells us this is the way to deepen our relationship with Jesus.

I began to realize more and more that I did not have to solve all problems. What a relief! I began to listen to my inner spirit (which is the dwelling place of the Holy Spirit) when decisions had to be made. Did the decision bring peace of mind about the situation? Or did it continually come back in questioning or doubting form? If it was the latter I began to understand this was probably self making the decision and I was not listening to or seeking enough guidance from the Holy Spirit.

I began to read books on prayer by Christian authors. (It is a good idea to run your list of books by your pastor, especially in the beginning. If you prefer, ask a Christian friend who knows Jesus on a personal level.) It is important that we read books based on Scripture by authors that are firmly entrenched in the love and truth of Jesus Christ.

I began to realize how very much God wants us to pray. When I first became involved in the prayer ministry I had such a small knowledge of the true power in prayer and what prayer does in us and for us. Prayer is one of the very special ways we can communicate with the Father. Prayers help people. Prayer is a very special gift from our Father. I believe God hears all our prayers. However, when we pray from a sense of pride, telling God exactly what we want and how we want it, we cannot expect God to fulfill our wishes. Why do I say that? Because God hears, but He knows what is really best for us. He answers our prayers according to His will for the situation at exactly the right moment. Usually those prayers that will make us look good to others or make life easier and gather more material things around us do not necessarily reflect what our Father desires for us.

God releases His power through prayer when we are praying without self at the forefront. The Lord desires our total concentration, desires our total surrender, our total repentance, our total love, our total trust. This sounds hard, doesn't it? But, believe me, we can do this with the help of the Holy Spirit. Did Jesus not say He was leaving but would give us another comforter? (John 14:15-17). This comforter, or counselor, will help you know the truths that Jesus spoke of. He will help you to run the great race. He will help you through the darkness into the light. The Holy Spirit in us is all truth, all love. His love is shiny and pure and creates a desire in us to be continually thankful and give our Father praise for His continual goodness. The Holy Spirit guides us into a deeper relationship with Jesus. What a very awesome gift we have been given.

CHAPTER 4

Visions, Insights, God's Word

During 1988 and 1989, I continued to grow in my love for Jesus, serving as ministry leader in prayer. Time and time again, I learned how much I did not know—but always the Holy Spirit was kind and gentle and led me through my mistakes or uncertainties to a better place. At the pastor's request, I began to help to put together praise services or special events at our church. I found myself hungering for times of praise to the Lord, a time when we could just sing choruses over and over and let the words wash over our entire beings. I would feel as if I were soaking in the warmth of God's love. To this day I continue to hunger for this kind of praise and worship.

I began to have visions of special meanings to ordinary things during a time of worship or prayer. I wondered what to do with them. People don't always want to hear about your vision. Over the years I have wondered why and have listened to many comments regarding this kind of situation. Is it a special gift for only a few? I really doubt it. But I do think we have to reach a point where we believe the words or visions are from God. We have to trust that the Holy Spirit will only give us words that are truth and, of course, those words will always be confirmed by scripture. We must weigh where and how we share what we have been given. And above all, we must give all glory to our Lord.

During a church leaders' retreat in January of 1990 I envisioned the following thoughts about giving praise to our Lord. As soon as I had this picture in my mind, I jotted down the thoughts that came with it as quickly as I could.

"Praise to you Lord is like a flower, a carnation. The outer petals are open, soft, simply defined. But the deeper you look into the middle of the flower, the tighter are the layers of petals, and in the very center of this tightness of the petals we experience the height of the delightful fragrance. Just so is our love for you. At first it seems light, easy, clearly defined. But as we reach deeper into our understanding of who You are, the tighter Your hold on us becomes, and the more complex our serving You becomes. Our desire to see more deeply into the very heart of Jesus continues to stretch us. We become more and more desirous of giving You praise and allowing Your Holy Spirit to guide us in worship and then the delightful fragrance of the Lord is poured into our very being. We are filled with a joy and peace beyond description.

When I wrote about the vision I just described in my journal that January, I made the notation "what a beautiful insight," and I truly believe it was a gift from the Holy Spirit, not something I could make up on my own. Many times I believe the Lord gives us these visions to increase our joy. They are like little warm fuzzies. I treasure these comparisons of our Lord to ordinary things in life. It reminds me of how everything is truly created by our God, so naturally all things can be compared in one way or another to God's love for the world.

The question has come to me many times about sharing or keeping still. Should we share these visions at the very moment we receive them? After many years of receiving visions and insights, and through trial and error of holding them close to my heart or sharing, I have found the following rules work best for me.

Sometimes yes. Other times I think we should wait. It has been eight years since I received the vision of the carnation, yet this seemed to be the right time to share it. Would it have meant as much if at that retreat I had gone from person to person sharing it eight years ago? Perhaps not. At that time it might have been seen by others as me bragging that I had "received a vision from the Lord" and they had not. It would have made me look good—and that is exactly what is not to happen in our serving—we don't look good, but our God looks good.

Learning to wait on the Lord's timing is difficult. I am a charge-ahead kind of person, so this has been a struggle for me (and is to this day). Yet I have found that God's timing is always perfect, whereas my timing is often far from the right time. I have been keeping notes on visions and thoughts received from the Lord as well as insights from scripture readings for more than fourteen years. When I need a special example for teaching or for comforting a person, quite often it is in my journals, just waiting for God's right time. I am constantly amazed at how perfectly something will fit a particular situation. I have learned to not fret over what I receive but to just enjoy it, read it over a few times, sometimes pray over it, and then file it away for when it will be needed. I share this with you because, dear reader, you might be one of these people who have all kinds of delightful insights and question what to do with them. Sometimes an insight can be worded in such a way that it does not sound preachy and can be offered for the church's newsletter. Perhaps you can share at times in a Sunday school class or prayer meeting. I definitely recommend writing them down in some form of a journal. What a wonderful way to brighten up a down day, by picking up your journal and reading back over a few months or a year all the wonderful things the Lord has brought to your mind. He is truly such a good God. There have been times when I have looked back through one of my journals and realized how God was using a particular situation to teach me and guide me into a closer relationship with Jesus. I probably did not even realize it at the time. You know, our Lord does this with us. He gives us a brief look into the window of a situation, then expects us to trust that He knows best and to just believe that whatever the end result, God is in ultimate control. I have seen this proven many times in my years of journaling. Believe me when I say it is not usually easy to say "Take over, Lord. I'll let you be in control. I'll just go along for the ride, whichever way You lead." We always think we have the best ideas and that we understand exactly what is needed. Have you been there? I fought letting God be in control of my life so many times. But each time that I finally say, "Take over Lord," the situation flows smoothly. Stress just disappears. Anxiety leaves.

I want to share some examples of Scripture insight. I wrote this in my journal, July 24, 1990:

As I was reading Eph. 1:3–6, the word "praise" leaped out for me. We are to give God praise because he gave us Jesus, through which we receive every spiritual blessing there is. What a gift, what love, and only through Jesus are we accepted as His. Again, the glory of this gift is to the praise of our Lord. This just reinforces my understanding that we are to praise our Lord all the day long, to acknowledge that all good things come from Him, whether it is in our personal lives, our work experiences, or in our special times of communicating with God. Since I believe current life is just a training ground for the life to come, we should be practicing the giving of praise for our very being to the one who loves us more than we can imagine. I visualize the giving of praise as God accepts it—not in an arrogant kingly acceptance—but a joyful radiance that is rather like a connecting rod between us and God and through which the power of the Lord (the Holy Spirit) is transferred."

And another insight from Eph. 1:6—8 the next day, July 25, 1990:

There are so many exciting words in these three verses, so full of meaning. There are action words such as "secured," "forgiven," "shedding," "lavished," "imparting." These five action words are all positive, all done by God for us. Jesus secured (held tight) our release (forgiveness) of sins by His shed blood (paid the ransom) on the cross. Our God has lavished gifts upon us, imparting His compassionate love in wonderful ways. Through the obedience of Jesus, we–God's children–can enjoy the richness of His gifts, all free—grace, wisdom, insight, and the sealing of the Holy Spirit indwelling in us. I have heard many times pastors and Christian speakers say God's love is free, no strings attached. Perhaps literally that is true, but I believe there are strings attached. To know Jesus, to love Him, to want to serve Him, creates conflict in our lives. It changes us, shifts our priorities, and if we do not seek His face, come to Him with our troubles, give Him praise each day of our lives, I do not believe we will know the ultimate joy of His wisdom, insight, love, and peace that waits for us as we live in this world.

I want to share just one more insight with you, which was also a vision. This came after reading the book of Hosea. In Hosea 14:8, God says, "I am the pine tree that shelters you." As I was sitting on the floor praying and looking out the family room window, I could see a huge pine tree, and the following vision came to me.

God's people are like the pine tree. All needles point upward, as do God's people who lift their hearts, their arms, their voices, their prayers, toward Heaven. The needles are thick, dense. As we give witness of our love and obedience to Jesus, as our example brings others into the fold, God's people multiply. The family of Christ becomes larger, a dense or greater concentration of believers.

Birds find haven from the elements in the thickness of the needles, the strong pliable branches. In the same way people can find haven from the worries of this world in Jesus' love, his protection from evil. The tree grows and grows, seeking nourishment from its roots. Just so, we receive nourishment when we have a relationship with Jesus. If our roots are firmly entrenched and we seek God's ways, we will grow in our love and trust and knowledge of Jesus. Fears will fall away. Joys will be uncovered and peace will fill our being. When the elements of evil beat against us, as the elements of nature do against the pine tree, we will be able to withstand their onslaught. The wind, the cold, the searing heat does not destroy the pine tree. Neither can the evils of this world destroy us when we love Jesus and are under His protection and seek Him for our shelter.

I wrote these insights nine to twelve years ago. These kinds of insights were completely new to me then. Do I still agree with them today? You bet I do. The Lord, by the guidance of the Holy Spirit, has changed me, my priorities have shifted—I spend time in prayer with Him each day of my life. I know He loves me, and I soak up the joy of His wonderful gift of peace.

I also receive joy from the words I hear in my spirit that create a type of poetry, or prose.

I have a whole folder of these poems. I use them periodically in my teaching. Sometimes I use one when I am writing prayer articles for our church newsletter. Often, after I copy my notes into hard copy, I read the poem again and am overwhelmed at the way the words flow together, and I know—am positive—that the words have been given to me at the direction of the Holy Spirit.

Let me give a word of caution here. Just because I mentioned earlier that my priorities have shifted, I spend time in prayer each day, listen for words from the Spirit, and give over my control in certain situations, this does not mean I am more spiritual or, as some people might say, "have arrived." Actually, the more I study, the more I pray, the more I give the Lord praise, the more I seek His guidance, the more I realize how much I still have to learn. I have only exposed the very outer layer of that which can be uncovered for a child of God. There is in me a sense of humility that He uses me when I know so little. I could give a long list of reasons why others would be better in serving the Lord in prayer, but He chose me, and there has been joy in this serving. I eagerly continue searching, studying, praying, praising, attending a conference occasionally, attending a special praise service periodically, all to bring me closer in my walk. Isn't it exciting to think this walk will never end? There is always the opportunity waiting for us to discover something new, deeper, or different about our Lord. I encourage you to never be content with where you are in your walk but always seek more, for there is a vast, almost indescribable amount of learning and experiencing waiting for us. Age does not have to be a factor, for I am no longer a young woman. Yet God, in His goodness, gives me stamina, enthusiasm, desire, expectation, and hunger to eagerly continue my walk with Him.

There are a couple of words I heard and did not understand when I first got involved in this new part of my life. Occasionally a man in our congregation would say "Amen" after a special song or prayer. I wondered why he did that.

I found out that the word "amen" means "so be it." Often today, I find myself saying "amen" after meaningful songs, prayers, or statements made by fellow believers.

Another phrase I noticed was "Praise the Lord." People around me said it a lot.

I thought it was kind of funny. Why would you tell someone about an incident and say, "Praise the Lord," with the other person nodding their head in agreement? Well, I found this was just another way of saying, "Thank you, Lord, for your goodness and the way You worked in the situation." It is a way of saying that God gets the glory. I feel comfortable using these expressions. In fact, they are part of my vocabulary now. However, when someone new comes into the fellowship of Jesus Christ, I pray I will be sensitive to the use of words that might be confusing to the person.

CHAPTER 5

There seems to be so much misunderstanding of how to accept the teachings from the Bible. Even though a person wants to be better, many are afraid to let go, to release control, to accept a spiritual realm of assistance. Of course, that spiritual assistance is the Holy Spirit. God always hears our prayers. However, I have learned that God often does not intervene in our reaching a decision or a choice. He gives us guidelines—many of them—but often our eyes are veiled or our ears plugged, and we make a choice that creates a consequence we don't like. Then we say, "Why did God allow this?"

Scripture tells us that God has given every person free will. This will not change. It is the choice of each individual to come to the Lord or to choose the darkness. By darkness I mean the ways of the secular world. God knows our hearts; He creates opportunities. He will and can open doors. He will love us regardless, but the final choice is always ours, and that is to make the choice God's way or the world's way.

Praying in faith (believing God is able to do all things) does help. There is a mystic quality of intangible strength that flows through us when we pray. This strength often touches the ones prayed for even though they are unaware. Continual prayer often softens the heart or creates the ability to hear or to reach out or to make wise decisions. Prayer is the best shield against the attacks of the evil one. It is the number one armament needed for the continual battle confronting a Christian. Of course, we always pray in the name of Jesus, because that name is the name that makes the demons tremble. And God loves us enough to allow us—actually gives us—the authority to use the name of Jesus in our prayers for protection. Remember, the name Jesus means "He who saves." As we build confidence in praying and making it a daily part of our lives, we begin to deepen our belief, love, gratitude, and humility before the Lord. There is nothing in this world more important then prayer, which is communicating with the Lord. God can build us up, encourage us, and guide us. When we turn to Him and deny our worldly ways, what does He do? He gives us the peace that floods our very being, that radiates from head to toe, that carries us through trials, that enables us to withstand suffering, that illuminates and grows our spirit. When this happens we start to tap the power of God that is released through us by the Holy Spirit. This power is great, but sadly most Christians do not reach out for it. There must be a complete willingness to always give God the glory for the results seen from prayer.

When the going gets tough and we are at our wits end trying to make the right choice, wouldn't taking time to ask our Heavenly Father to intervene or to give us guidance or to quiet our trembling hearts be a good choice? But how often do we do this? Instead, we choose a course, try to fix the situation in our own strength, and then quite often watch the whole thing crash around us. Is this God's fault? No. We choose. He did not make us robots or puppets. That would have been simple. God wants us to be His friends, His loving, dedicated servants. He wants us to desire His wisdom and His guidance for our lives. Over and over, Scripture instructs us to ask, seek, repent, forgive, come. That is exactly what we can do in prayer. This is our choice to allow God to run the show. Sometimes walking through the situation is hard. God does not promise us it will be easy. But He does promise to be with us, to never leave us, to help us through the situation.

Probably, most of us are confronted with daily decisions—some easy and some difficult. Often a decision or choice presents a dilemma for us. Scripture tells us that if we lack wisdom we should ask God for help. In other words, pray. And I quote: "If any of you lacks wisdom, he should ask God, who gives generously to all without finding fault, and it will be given to him. But when he asks, he must believe and not doubt..." (James 1:5-6a).

Seeking God's will and direction in relinquishing our will, our own choice, makes us ready and receptive to hear Him and obey. The above scripture says when we ask we must believe and not doubt. This means we not only believe in the existence of God but we also believe in His loving care. We believe He will hear and answer our prayer, perhaps not in the way we view it, but He will answer. We must remember God does not answer every selfish or thoughtless request. Our hope and expectation is that God will align our desires with His purposes. Praying for small daily decisions prepares us to seek our God when the big decisions come along. We are then conditioned to choose to seek God's desire for the situation.

This choice to seek God's will for a situation is actually the act of surrendering our own control. The world teaches we should have control of our lives; that a macho person will always be in control of any situation confronting him or her. But God says (and we know His Word is truth), "Trust the Lord with all your heart ..." (Prov. 3:5). This means to bring the situation to Him through prayer for help, for strength, and for courage to carry out His solution over our own human desires. God promises to keep our paths straight when we seek His will, His way, and not our own. This does not mean we will always get the answer we want. Sometimes the troubles seem to deepen as we pray, but the end result of our prayer is a closer relationship with Jesus, more trust in the mercy and love of our Heavenly Father, and a richer understanding of the ministering power of the Holy Spirit through Christ Jesus. The power of the Holy Spirit is released through us and in us as we surrender ourselves.

I mentioned that I had been journaling since 1986. One Sunday in June of 1990, Rev. Jerry Kirk, former pastor of a large Presbyterian church and a man who was instrumental in establishing a ministry for the National Coalition for Protection of Children and Families, was the guest speaker at our church. He challenged us to start reading a few verses of scripture each day and then journal what these verses spoke to us. I thought about this for a couple of weeks and then decided in July to try it. I selected the book of Ephesians. So now not only do I have journals of my thoughts and experiences, I also have journals of a good many books of the Bible. How helpful these Bible study journals have been in my teaching over the years. When I started doing this, the last thought in my mind was that some day I would share these thoughts with others. Yet here I am, years later, sharing with you some of the eye-opening thoughts I had from July 23, 1990, in my journal of Ephesians. No doubt, you have gathered that I like the book of Ephesians.

A Prisoner of Christ Jesus

In Eph. 3:1-2, Paul says he is a prisoner of Christ Jesus. What do you suppose he means by that? First, a prisoner is someone who has been captured, put into submission, who serves the desires of the captor, put into involuntary restraint. Perhaps Paul meant he became a prisoner of Christ Jesus at the beginning of his ministry by our Lord calling to him and laying such a heavy burden on his heart. I don't think Jesus makes us involuntary prisoners, but I do believe that the more we know Jesus, the more we serve Him, the more we love Him, the more we become prisoners. Because our hearts are softened by His great love for us, and we are so filled with the Holy Spirit, there is no turning back to the way we were before. If this is being a prisoner, then I am glad Jesus captured me.

Remember, I mentioned earlier that I believe there are strings attached when we accept Jesus as our Lord and Savior. In Eph. 4:1-3 we are entreated to live up to God's calling for us:

- be humble always
- gentle
- patient
- forbearing with one another
- charitable
- make fast with bonds of peace the unity which the Spirit gives

These things don't sound hard to do, but lumped together they are very hard, or at least to me they seemed hard to fulfill. These are areas I struggle with continually. It calls for constant vigilance on our parts, battling against our egos, our selfishness, and our tunnel vision of self. It goes back to the desire of wanting to be a prisoner of Jesus. If we allow this desire to surface and become our most important focus, will we not strive to do the above? Even if we stumble, God is merciful and understanding, for He knows our hearts, He knows if we are sincere.

Again, in Eph. 4:7-8 Paul states, "....when Jesus ascended on high he led captives in his train...." Notice again the reference to prisoners. But I don't visualize these captives as downtrodden, beaten, dragging their feet, chained and hurting, with hopelessness registered in their eyes. Rather these prisoners–and hopefully I am one of them–are in a train or line of captives with joyful looks, eagerness, a lilt to their steps, gentleness, and contentment as they follow Jesus. One can sense adoration pouring forth from the sounds of their voices and they radiate the reflected light of Jesus in their contacts with all people.

We must remember there is no mention of "prisoners of Christ" being only one kind of people. God loves all the world, and His greatest desire is for all people to come to know Jesus. This is the unity mentioned often in the Bible. Beginning to understand what this unity meant moved me to another whole area of thinking about the love of Christ and my role as His prisoner. Journaling as I read a verse or two of Scripture each morning before I went to work drew me into thinking seriously about God's Word. I believe it taught me to stop doubting and to start believing more deeply that this book held the secret to my fears.

My goal was to become a mature Christian, which according to this chapter of Ephesians is measured by the fullness of our acceptance and understanding of Christ Jesus. Does this sound like another easy hurdle? It is quite the opposite, at least for me. It takes a lifetime of dedication, obedience, trust, prayer, selflessness, and shifting priorities. But the price is not too much to know Jesus, to understand even a little what God wills for us. The joy, the peace that flows through us, is a great reward and we are promised those rewards will be greater to come.

Paul, in his letter to the Ephesians, continues by saying that when we utilize the gifts God gives us we become a vital part of the body as a whole. Each of us has a role to play in creating this bond built on love with Jesus as the head of the body. What a beautiful thought.

It is like building with a child's Legos®. Each piece connects with another. The more you connect and build the pieces together, the stronger the structure becomes, and from starting with one little rectangle, something of interest, something new is formed. However if one Lego® is removed, it weakens the structure or leaves a hole. So it is when we don't respond to God's call for us. When we concentrate on self rather than others we weaken the structure of our sustaining faith and leave a hole for the enemy to infiltrate into our lives.

Another example would be to compare God's power to a rivet. Rivets are used to hold a structure together. The rivets are there, unnoticed by most, and taken for granted. It is that way with God's power. Most of us take it for granted. If God pulled that power away, it would be like pulling the rivets out of the building; the whole structure would crumble. Do we shackle God's power? Does our unbelief put up barriers to the release of God's power? What about our lack of trusting God and our unwillingness to be humble and submissive before Him? Do these kinds of actions or lack of actions hold back the releasing of God's power in our churches and in our personal lives? It is rather overwhelming to think that we make the choice every single day of whether or not to allow God to be all He can be. Do you want to be a prisoner of Christ, or would you rather be a prisoner to the things of this world? We choose, and what we choose results in either being filled with the peace that only God can give or being in a continual state of anxiety in some form or other.

These are some of the thoughts I had written and decided to share with you. There are so many—actually notebooks full. This was a great teaching tool for my beginning to understand what God's Word speaks to each of us. I continued journaling books of the Bible for several years, actually through December of 1993. It was a great learning experience, and it opened my eyes to what I had been missing in not studying the Word of God. This was the beginning of my longing for a deeper understanding and clarity of what God was saying to me through His Word. Someone once said that studying the Word of God and accepting His truths was a form of receiving love letters from the Lord. Pretty neat! I hope by this time I have whetted your appetite to read on and find out more about what God in His goodness and mercy has done for me, just one of his children.

CHAPTER 6

Sustaining Faith

I want to tackle an area I have struggled with for a long time. When things have gotten rough, often someone would say to me, "Just have faith," or "Don't you have faith?" This always put me on the defensive. I would think, *Apparently I don't have faith, so how do I get it?* Actually, at times it even irritated me because I did not know how to answer. I have learned there is a lesson here for me. I have wondered why some people seem to have faith that all will work out, or they just never question what is happening, or they use the famous line, "I just have faith."

Over the years, my Bible studies have helped me immeasurably to understand more about what faith is and what faith is not. I should clarify I am talking about faith that sustains us. Of course, God gives us the faith that saves when we accept Jesus as our Lord and Savior. But in our daily living we need faith to see us through difficulties, uncertainties, and what I call the low times. I don't think this sustaining faith is something you go to God in prayer and ask for and it suddenly is there. I believe it is striving to live each day with the fruits of the spirit (gentleness, caring, kindness, purity, love, etc.). It is studying God's Word and praying that the Holy Spirit will reveal the truth to our understanding. It is admitting a trust in God's power and surrendering our will to God's will.

I think some people appear to have more faith because they have learned to trust God. Perhaps they don't even realize on a conscious level the extent of their trust, but I believe for our faith to be strong, we have to trust God. Note I did not say trust *in* God, I said trust God. I want to describe sustaining faith as I have come to understand it.

It is knowing and believing:

- Without any question that God is!
- That God can do anything He desires, anything.
- That Jesus will come again, no question, He will.
- That Jesus will make the final judgment and those God chooses will be with Him forever.
- That God can move mountains, divide waters, and raise the dead.
- There is absolutely nothing He cannot do.
- That He loves unconditionally, not with rules or regulations.
- That when His power is unleashed it is beyond what we can imagine.
- That there are always hosts of God's angels standing ready at all times to do battle in the heavenlies or spiritual realms even though we cannot see them.
- That God's heavenly kingdom spreads far and wide beyond anywhere man can know.

There was a time I would have questioned many of these statements. There was a time I would have argued that they were impossible. Now I know these statements are only a beginning of who God is and what He can do. Sustaining faith is believing when others try to make us doubt God's abilities. Sustaining faith is believing even when circumstances seem to create doubt of God's presence. Sustaining faith is believing God loves me even when I goof up. Sustaining faith is knowing that I am part of the royal priesthood of believers (1 Pet. 1:9), that I belong to God, and that Jesus paid the price for my freedom.

So back to the question of how one gets sustaining faith for daily living. First, be hungry to seek God. Profess belief in Jesus and hunger to study His Word. Pray, pray, and pray for the Holy Spirit to reveal all truth to your mind and heart. Be in fellowship with other believers. Seek opportunities to praise God in worship services. Turn away from those things the Holy Spirit tells you are not of God. Suddenly, you will realize the statements I made before take on new meaning. You probably could add many more. Putting these thoughts into practice will bring a release, a freshening to your spirit, a joy to your heart, beyond description. Does this come quickly? Perhaps for some people, but for me it has taken many years. It was 1991 that those statements started being true for me and even now, all these years later, I continue to elaborate on them. It is worth all the effort, all the struggles, all the study, all the praying, all the questioning, to receive the freedom of saying with joy, "Yes, I have faith—the faith of salvation because of the Cross of Calvary. And a sustaining faith for any circumstances that come my way, because I know that God loves me."

But God didn't just give this sustaining faith to me. I had to grow in understanding. I had to take time away from worldly pleasures to seek what the Lord wanted me to realize about Him. I had to start trusting God, admitting He knows better than I how to handle situations. In other words, I had to surrender my pride and my time. Then God could be what He says He is. This meant changing my concepts of how big God was at the beginning of time as we know it and how big God is at this very moment and forever. This meant allowing the Holy Spirit to bring to the surface those things I had previously thought were right and admit that many were false beliefs or perhaps, more accurately, confused beliefs. And this meant admitting I didn't know it all. Another blow to my ego. God does love to make one humble, I think.

We are reminded that life is not a bed of roses as we moan or complain about difficulties we face. In 1 Peter 1:6-7 we are told we may come under trials at times. We should expect this. This fallen world is full of snares and temptations to live as the world says is good rather than trusting that God knows best. When our sustaining faith stands the test, we are told it is more precious than gold. I think it is very difficult to hold fast to faith when things are darkest. It is much easier to sing God's praises when things are going well.

In 1 Pet. 2:4—10 we are told that Jesus is the living stone. He was rejected by men but chosen by God, and is precious to Him. Jesus is the cornerstone of our faith. As we accept Jesus, we become living stones, and we are being built into a spiritual house, for God's kingdom is in our hearts. We then become a holy priesthood of believers, offering spiritual sacrifices that are acceptable to God through Christ Jesus. How do we do this? Through our faith in believing in Jesus. Otherwise, Jesus becomes a stumbling rock to trip over, and those without faith will fall. Isn't it exciting to realize we have been called out of darkness (that is the worldly ways) into the light of the world, our Lord Jesus?

Each step we take in our search to know Jesus better is a step closer to receiving more of this sustaining faith. God promises to help us through temptations and trials. He promises us eternal life through His Son, Jesus. The rest is up to us. It is our choice.

It always comes back to our choice. He never forces us. Once we make the choice to follow Jesus, to establish a personal relationship with Him, there is no turning back. We set our feet on His path, our eyes focused outwardly (toward others), not inwardly (toward self) as the world tells us to do. In making that choice we can anticipate continual spiritual growth and understanding of the inspired words of God through the guidance of the Holy Spirit. This in turn deepens our sustaining faith. We must have patience in our growing. We will no doubt stumble at times, but God will help us if we continue to turn to Him. If we have heard the good news of Jesus, if we profess to believe, if we begin to pray, if we say we love the Lord—and then are too lazy to seek more truths, to follow His will, to put others before ourselves, to give witness to His glory and praise to Jesus—how can we expect God to fulfill His promises to us? We will stagnate, and I believe with all my heart we will not know the deep abiding joy that Jesus promised.

You might say that eternal life is God's gift, no strings attached. But when a gift is offered it has to be accepted. When you are given a gift, do you leave it in the box on a shelf in a dark corner, forgotten, perhaps looked at occasionally, but never used? Or do you take the gift out of the box, use it, enjoy it, and allow it to be a constant reminder of the giver?

Here are our choices when God gives so freely:

- We receive, or we reject.
- We accept, or we mock.
- We honor, or we dishonor.
- We praise Him, or we praise ourselves.
- We love Him, or we love self.
- We seek Him, or we seek self-adulation.

The choice is ours. Faith deepens as we choose to receive, accept, honor, praise, love, and seek more of our Heavenly Father in Jesus.

How exciting! I have always loved a challenge. And I have never had such a challenge as coming to know Jesus and finding I have talents that were untapped by worldly expectations. I love the scripture that says "I can do all things through Christ who strengthens me" (Phil. 4:13). What kind of choices are you making?

Nothing Hidden

Do you remember when I told you about my dad and how Jesus helped me walk through all the hurt I was holding inside? After that, I figured I really had it all together. There were no longer barriers to keep me from deeper contact with the Lord—or so I thought. However, over the years, the Lord continued to bring to the surface areas that I needed to work on. About 1995, Mother's eyes weakened to the point I had to do all her bookwork. The healing never left. She was always able to take care of herself and could see to do things, but reading became too difficult. My dear mother and I seemed to have quite a bit of trouble communicating. I often felt that nothing I did really pleased her. She wanted to make me into whatever it was she pictured me to be. I prayed for mother to accept me as I was, not to criticize me so much, to give me credit for having a good measure of common sense, but nothing was changing. It was just getting worse. During one of my prayer times—or quiet times as I often call them—I started reflecting and knew I had forgiven my real father for leaving me as a baby. He was young, perhaps weak, perhaps overwhelmed with responsibility. I probably will never know, but it is no longer important. But how must Mother have felt? It could not have been easy to be rejected with a little baby to be responsible for. She had never worked and suddenly had no money. She returned to her parents' home and lived under their rules. She is a fair person, and she always tries to please others. It was revealed to me that after she married my stepdad, she probably believed I knew she loved me. Therefore she lavished her love on my three step-sisters because she felt they had a rough time early in their lives. Of course, she never knew that it hurt me. She never knew I felt I was always last because I did not have a daddy and I had to share my mother.

As I wrote these words in my journal later, I realized I had never expressed these thoughts to anyone. I didn't even realize I was harboring these kinds of thoughts. I knew then that I must forgive my mother and then forgive myself for the emotions and feelings that had built up over a very long time. A child often twists situations, thinks concretely, and sees only that black is black and white is white. Gray does not exist. As adults we realize there is much gray in our lives.

So if I ask forgiveness, what is the next step? It is to accept what is and learn how to live with that. I must not shove all these resentments and misunderstandings into the corner of my mind or my heart, but must put them behind me. How do I do this? Jesus has assured us that if we lay our burdens at the cross, He will carry them for us. So I did that. I said, "Right now, Lord, I lay all these things at the foot of the cross—the pains, the hurt, the rejection, the anger, the bitterness, the resentment." Yes, I felt all those emotions. "I now know, Lord, none of these things would my mother have wanted me to believe she imparted to me. Perhaps, Lord, my wanting to be first in her life, wanting her praise, is not to be. Lord, help me to accept that. Help me to be kind, caring, and a loving daughter, not sarcastic or impatient. Help me remember to treat her as I would want my daughters to treat me. Help me to be more honest with her, more open in my feelings. Lord, I thank you for helping me work through this. Thank you for opening my eyes to that which I have held deep inside me for so long."

Reader, do you see what the Holy Spirit was teaching me? My prayer was no longer "Change my mother." It was "Change me." Did it work? Yes. Not completely at that moment, but it was a start. I think that was the first time I truly understood what it means to give my burdens to Jesus. It has taken me several years to completely let go of the resentment caused by her remarks and to enjoy my times more with mother. She still bosses me around, expecting me to be her precious little girl. Sometimes when I express my feelings about a situation, she will say; "Well, I just don't believe that. You can't possibly feel that way." So my prayers are definitely being answered in my changed attitude, not my mom's. But funny as it may seem, that is okay now. Of course, I would like to hear her express support for me more often, but apparently this is hard for her. She does thank me for helping her and tells me how much she loves me. I am coming to terms with this and trying to accept that Mom is probably never going to change. Whoops! Does God answer prayer? I reached another milestone with Mom in the year, 2001. We spent a Sunday afternoon and evening together having a good time, eating, and hashing over our memories. She gave me an envelope when I took her home. Later, when I read it, all the things I have been writing and sharing with you were covered in this note. She wrote how very proud she is of me, how very thankful that she has me as her daughter. She thanks God so often that we are able to be together, and she loves me very much, and she gave me some money to spend for my golf outings. I called her to thank her for the gift and then told her how important the note was to me and that I would save it forever. Her comment was, "Why Evelyn, don't you know I love you?"

Learning this lesson has helped me in dealing with many kinds of situations in the years since the Lord helped me work through this. We cannot change others, but God helps us change ourselves. When *we* are willing—and I emphasize when we are willing—to let Him change us, then He can heal memories, hurts, or whatever. But if we are not willing to change, how can we expect to be healed? For Jesus taught us in the Lord's Prayer to say, "Forgive us our debts, as we also have forgiven our debtors" (Matt. 6:12). The condition seems to be that when we have forgiven others, we can seek and expect forgiveness for ourselves. Our prayer then is one of coming before the Lord in humility, repentance, leaning on His mercy, goodness, and compassion.

Our God is so good. He never fails in helping us through the problem. I can truthfully say that the hurts are gone. The resentment is gone. I can hear the hurtful remarks now and just laugh. Well, to be totally honest, occasionally the hurt or resentment pops up again. But now I know how to give the feelings to Jesus and say to myself, *This is just Mom's way.* And the strangest thing of all is how often my mom says, "I'm so proud of you Sally (her pet name for me). I love you, you are dear to me."

A few years after I went through this letting go, Mom said something to me that really irritated me. I didn't say anything to her, but I went home and fumed about her sarcastic remarks. This was one of the days when I couldn't laugh it off easily. At this point, I now know I had better pray about the feelings. So I went to my special spot and spouted off my feelings. Hear is what I heard in my spirit.

Your relationship with your mother is deep-rooted from when you were a little child. You felt different. Not only was your dad gone, but your mother was not there either. This affects a child in ways no one can explain. For you it created resentment. And, yes, that is the word that is harbored deep down in your subconscious. But, Evelyn, you were always loved. Times were hard. Your mother did the best she could. She was young and protected and also rejected and hurt, embarrassed and shamed by her standards. She is a completely different type personality than you. You are much like your father.

Well, as I read the words I had hastily written down, it made me really think. Mom was raised in the times when divorce was not an everyday occurrence. She came from a family that had been well-to-do. She had never worked outside the home. I guess I never thought about her feelings and how she always hid them away, never talking about them. It gave me a whole new perspective on our relationship. So even though I previously thought all the feelings were gone, still there were some harbored deep within. God cleared out the cobwebs. He is such an awesome God.

Mom is ninety-five years old as I write this, so I am very blessed that this could be resolved while she is still here. I don't want you to think there are no more challenges coming from Mom. There always are. I have come to realize it is hard for Mom to accept my independence from her. She wants to be needed. She wants to make decisions. She has never understood that love allows freedom. But since my attitude has changed from being defensive to trying to understand her, I can just chuckle or change the subject or, as in the current lingo, refuse to go there. But I also tell her I love her and that she is my favorite mom.

Another point I want to share with you that I have learned from studying Scripture is that nothing is hidden from God. He knew how I felt deep inside even though I had never expressed it aloud. He knew I needed this release. So when I was willing to let it go and listen and accept, the Lord removed it. It is much more difficult to serve our Lord willingly and easily when we are holding resentments or bitterness or unresolved anger or hurts within ourselves. God knows this and, as we desire more and more to have a deeper relationship with Jesus, He begins to weed out these repressed feelings. It is interesting how this does not necessarily happen—or at least for me—all at once but has continued over a period of years. Each time something was brought to the surface of my mind, I was ready to deal with it. And this is, I believe, because the Holy Spirit, indwelling in me, sensed I was ready to take another step in releasing my control to the control of the Holy Spirit. The freedom is indescribable.

The perspective from which I now work through things with my mom is completely different. Did Mom change through my prayers about the whole situation? Not much. But the Holy Spirit changed me!

This is an important lesson in growing in Jesus, to understand that we are not fooling Him at all in denying what is buried deep in our hearts. We might as well get it out in the open to Him. Turn to Him for help, acknowledging that we cannot deal with the situation by ourselves. That's really all God asks us to do. Scripture tells us to "Lean on Him and not on our own understanding," "He will help us through all the difficulties" (Prov. 3:5-6; 1 Cor. 10:13).

I am fairly sure there are more things hidden deep in the recesses of my mind that the Lord will weed out as the years continue to flow by. But now I rest assured that I will be able to deal with whatever the Lord brings to my awareness, because He will be with me. Isn't that a comfort?

How I wish I had learned that sooner! Perhaps writing this for others to read will help someone make that decision right now. Even as I am writing this and remembering how my relationship with Mom was and how it is now, it just blows me away. How awesome is our God! How awesome is His acceptance of a relationship with us.

What is it about a personal relationship with Jesus that is different from a personal relationship with anyone else? We cannot see Him; we cannot touch Him. Yet He draws us to the mystery of who He is—a man, a spirit, the Creator who always was, who is, and who always will be. This is so far beyond our comprehension. Why do we desire or even think it is possible to know Him? There seems to be a deep-down hunger for acceptance in all of us, a desire for someone to love us just as we are, for someone to enjoy us without continually wanting or expecting us to be what we are not. We humans cannot seem to love without conditions. Doesn't it seem we love others and accept them when they do as we desire, yet not love and accept them just as they are?

But this Jesus is different. He already knows our faults, our hesitancies, our doubts, our fears, our bravado, the façade we present to the world. Yet He loves us, opens His arms to us. He welcomes us into His kingdom just as we are. This acceptance is so humbling, so overwhelming in its vastness, that it draws us as a magnet. We pull back—yet step forward. We turn away—then turn back. Nothing else seems to satisfy. Nothing can take the place of that unconditional acceptance of our most inner self.

And this Jesus who saves, who loves, who laid down His life willingly for each of us so that our mistakes, our imperfections, our selfishness, which is part of our sinful nature, could be forgotten just as though they never happened, loves us this much. Our hunger for acceptance creates in us an awe, a feeling of *How could I be important enough? What have I ever done to be considered good enough to have a relationship with Jesus?* Of course, we are not worthy. But Jesus' death on the cross and God's grace allows us to eagerly, with humility, love, devotion, and thankfulness, enter into this never ending relationship with Jesus, the only Son of the most high God. Age has no meaning; it is not a hindrance. Man, woman, child, it makes no difference. Each of us is equally important to the Lord. Each of us was lost, but when we accept Jesus and start on that journey of discovery that He alone is our very best friend, our confidant, our redeemer—then we are found. And there is a joy that fills our very being. That joy floods our hearts. It tingles in our bodies. It radiates through our eyes, our voices. It shows in our compassion for others, our willingness to give of ourselves with no expectation of return. We shed tears of joy because mere words cannot express the love Jesus pours into us by His Holy Spirit. To know this, to accept it, to desire it beyond anything else in this world is a precious gift. How very much we are loved.

A word of caution here, dear reader; from what you have just read please don't feel as though you could never reach this point or if you have, that's all there is. First, let me assure you if the Lord can do such a radical change in me, He can do a change in you also. Secondly, He is still working on me. Every time I think now it should be easier. Zap! Another layer of something that is not pleasing to the Lord is revealed to me, another area for me to work on. I can only assure you that even though at times I really don't want to work on another change because I like what I am doing, when I am obedient to His desire for me to change, in the end it becomes another step of freedom. We are such perverse people. We like to stay in our habit mode where we are comfortable. But our God continually creates in us new hearts, changed ways, drawing us closer to Him. I have come to believe that as long as I am living in this world, our wonderful Lord will continue to change me, teach me, and reveal to me new revelations of His goodness. Remember earlier when I was talking about gifts? In 1997 the following poem came to me during my prayer time with the Lord.

My Gift to You

My gift does not come in a box
Lined with tissue, wrapped in beautiful paper
Or tied with a fancy ribbon.
My gift is not something to put on a shelf.
It is something that will never go out of style.
My gift is one that endures, it endures forever.
For it is the gift of life eternal.
This gift is given you through devotion to Christ Jesus.
By accepting Him and believing in Him,
You have opened the gift
And recognized the treasure within.
The more you use this gift

The more you will realize how precious it is.
For it will take away fear and hopelessness,
Loneliness, anger, resentment.
This gift replaces all negative feelings
With love and joy and peace.
And the sure knowledge that I love you,
That Jesus Christ loves you,
That the Holy Spirit is ever present in you,
And that you will be with us in eternity.
Enjoy your gift.
I love to see my children receive this gift
And allow it to be the treasure of their hearts.

Written Nov. 15, 1997

CHAPTER 7

The Enemy

Much is spoken in the Bible about Satan. We are told he was one of God's most beautiful angels—the angel of light—who decided he wanted the power that God had. So now he is a fallen angel, an implacable enemy of God, and a malicious adversary of God's people. Because of the sin of mankind in the Garden of Eden, Satan has control over this world until the return of Jesus. I don't intend to go into all the suppositions of how Satan became the temporary ruler of the world or exactly how this happened. I just want to focus on how we can make the darts of the enemy, which are really there, harmless. We are given so many guidelines on how to pray for protection. We are given the authority to cast out evil in the name of Jesus and to resist evil by submitting to God (James 4:7). We are given the armor of protection in Ephesians 6:13-18. Would all of this be necessary if Satan was not real?

There is no need to fear our enemy, Satan, the evil one. But we need to be wary. He does lurk everywhere. He wants to destroy God's kingdom, which is in the hearts of God's people. Satan's ways are very deceptive. That which looks and feels good is not always of God. It can be a covering for an evil situation or temptation the enemy places before us. I cannot stress enough how important it is for every single believer in Jesus to pray each and every day for protection from the evil one, Satan.

It can be a simple prayer such as: "Lord, protect me this day from anything the enemy would try to put against me. In the name of Jesus."

We are told the enemy is powerful, but God is more powerful. The only time Satan can win over God is when we allow it. What do I mean by that? Simply that when something unpleasant happens in our lives, we tend to say, "Well, that's the breaks." Or we fall into despair or we become bitter or angry. This is exactly what Satan wants us to do. But what does God tell us we should do? Pray! Give God praise for what we do have. Lift up the name of Jesus in praise. We are to praise God in all things—not *for* all things but *in* all things. (I Peter 4:11)

In our prayers we should state aloud—I say aloud because the enemy cannot read our thoughts—that we rebuke whatever the enemy is trying to do in our lives. Of course, always pray in the name of Jesus. Immediately after the rebuke, tell the Lord we love Him, we praise Him, and we believe all things are possible with the almighty God. We are told Satan trembles at the name of Jesus. The demons wither and flee because they know Jesus is God's Son. I use this simple prayer over and over when things seem to be out of sync or I feel harried. And afterwards I feel a sense of peace and calmness.

Remember, it is only through belief in Jesus that we can overcome the negative thoughts, ideas, and situations that are placed before us in this world. Satan will continually create new ways to make us think God has deserted us. I believe Satan knows our weaknesses because he watches our actions, our responses to situations. Yet we are told over and over that God cares about us. We know this is true because John 3:16 tells us that God so loved the world He gave His only son to die for our sins, and by professing belief in Jesus we can have eternal life.

Now think about it. Would Satan be unhappy about this? Would he try everything he could think of to confuse us? Would he try to entice us with things that focus on self, greed, or on that which offends the Holy Spirit? Sounds logical to me.

As an example, my home has nine rooms. Yet at one point several years ago I kept longing for a bigger house—more area to put "stuff." Possibly, deep down inside, I wanted to impress my friends with how lovely everything was. I thought about how I could change things, add more living space. One morning during my prayer time, I started praying for the homeless people. I prayed about how they must feel, what they do not have, wondering how they stand it. Then I thought, *why am I praying about this? What has brought this to my consciousness so vividly?* In my heart the words just started tumbling out. *Look around, I have so much. What if it was all taken away from me? Is this not enough? Where is my focus—on worldly things, right? And where should it be? On the things that relate to what our Lord wants for me.* Immediately I knew that Satan was trying to confuse me, to distract me from the work the Lord has called me to do. I was being drawn into worldly values, impressing others with what I had.

We need to be aware of the insidious ways the enemy tries to pull us away from God. He covers his lies in fancy trappings, but they are not the really important things in life. The important things are caring about others, loving our Lord and communicating with Him, helping those in need, praying for others, trusting in Jesus, spreading the message of Jesus, bringing others to the point of salvation where they will desire to know Jesus, spending each day in the sure knowledge that we are loved by God, who wants only good things for us. When we focus on this, I assure you that the peace and joy of the Lord flows through us. Satan and his lies are defeated.

There are many false spirits that will try to trap us into believing a lie. The spirit of ridicule can cause division between brother and sister or between friends, co-workers, or husband and wife. It can create agitation between mother and father for the child. This, in turn, opens the door for the spirit of rebellion to become evident. The spirit of doubt can cause one to be defeated in accepting a new challenge of life. Doubt can cause one to feel discouraged, depressed, lethargic, or incapable of accomplishing the task. All negative thoughts are from the enemy. The enemy does not want us to succeed in anything that would draw us closer to God. He does not want us to love God, to worship God, to be a witness for Jesus Christ, or to be a follower of Jesus. The enemy will always fight to keep us from choosing God in the only way he can; he will try to confuse us with negative false beliefs of our love for the Lord. Some of these false beliefs include confusion, doubt, unworthiness, apathy, discouragement, violent anger, criticism, jealousy, and greed. Each one of these false beliefs takes us into an area of disruptive behavior. We are focusing on the deterrents of living, not on the joy-filled promises of our Lord.

There will always be times of trouble, because the enemy is never still, never satisfied, never asleep. Just as God's Word says, Satan prowls like a hungry lion waiting to destroy our dreams and plans and lives any way he can (1 Pet. 5:8). At other times we say we are too busy to do something for the Lord. We get into a comfortable routine. It looks innocent, yet the enemy subtly keeps us from becoming closer to God because of the comfort we take in our routine. What happens? We become trapped into a mode of inertia.

We need to rebuke Satan when negative thoughts of any kind come to our minds. We must not allow him room in our thoughts. He is not worthy to be near us. Because even though he was called the angel of light, he is no longer the light but is the darkness. He is doomed. He wants to be the victor, but it will never be. Jesus' death and resurrection made Jesus victorious over evil. Satan is the defeated foe of God's people. That is God's promise. When we fail to recognize this on a daily basis, negative thoughts start swirling around and often penetrate our minds. One of the wonderful things about prayer is our understanding, believing, and knowing it is a force Satan cannot stop. Each time a prayer is spoken, a false, evil spirit cringes and sometimes crumbles. Barriers are weakened. At one time I never gave much thought to the devil (as I used to think of him). But as my walk with the Lord has deepened, as my desire to serve the Lord has increased, and as my prayer life has become so much a part of me every day, my awareness of the enemy has increased.

There truly is always a battle going on between our focus on God and our focus on this world. Satan is a tough adversary. He does not give up willingly or easily. His snares are many. They can look like a pebble on the road and yet be as difficult to walk around or over as a boulder. We must remember the enemy delights in discouraging us and in pulling us away from focusing on the Lord. He knows nothing of goodness, of kindness, or caring about people. Satan's goal—his only goal—is to prove that his power is greater than God's power. He does not care at all about us as individuals. It is only because God desires us to be His that Satan wants to pull us into his bondage. Then Satan can say, "Look, God, see what my power can do?" So is it about us? No. It is about power—Satan's versus God's. We are the players tossed about in this continual battle. Does God want this? No. Does Satan want this? Yes. It should be very clear who is really for us. We need to watch out for Satan's tricks. His ways are subtle. He will try anything to cause confusion, to create doubt, to make us feel unworthy, to make us feel apathy or discouragement. Beware of his ploys.

When we allow the lures and the lies of Satan to trap us, we are lined up on the side of the enemy, and our reward for this is only the desires and standards set by the world's goals. What happens? We can become enslaved to these wants and goals and, even worse, we become negative in our response to situations around us. We start thinking it is fate or that we are just unlucky, etc. Not true. Jesus is the victor. Believe in Jesus and know Satan has no right to you.

You are probably wondering whether I still long for a bigger house. Yes, at times I do, especially when the whole family is together. Twenty-some people can fill up a 16 x 20 family room quickly. My grandkids think it is "so fun" to climb over one another to get from one room to the next at Christmas gatherings. Joyful bedlam. But the Holy Spirit has made me aware that what I have is really enough, and when I start longing for more, I remind myself I could have less. When these thoughts of wanting more come (and where do you think they come from?) I just offer praise to our Lord that He has supplied all my needs in abundance. The more I give praise to the Lord for all that I have, the more I tend to enjoy the things I have and to feel satisfied. I believe God blesses us when we give Him praise in all things. I have seen this happen over and over. What a wonderful, loving God we have.

It is pretty awesome to think how prayer can change things. Of course, it is not we who change things, only God can do that. But our prayers are needed to create the atmosphere for the change to happen, and that can be our desires, our attitudes, our hopes, our outlooks, or our understanding. Prayer is the best defense we have against the enemy. God has provided a way for us to be overcomers of Satan's ploys on a daily basis. Remember what I said during the last chapter? Nothing is hidden from God. But God waits for us to turn to Him. How patient He is. In the next chapter I will explain the many ways I have seen prayer work for good and how it helps me stay focused on my walk with the Lord.

CHAPTER 8

The Joy of Praying

This chapter covers a number of different ways of praying. I will explain the learning curve I experienced over the many years of my walk with the Lord in prayer. What benefits do we derive from giving God a specific amount of time in prayer each and every day? I have found prayer gives us so many benefits. Actually, I would call them, blessings.

- Prayer draws us closer to God.
- Prayer helps us understand Him better.
- Prayer helps us realize how deeply God loves us.
- Prayer allows us to appreciate the gift of Jesus more.
- Prayer helps us realize the power of the Holy Spirit working in us and through us to God's glory.
- Prayer gives us new understanding of humility.
- Prayer allows us to receive joy and fulfillment beyond expression.
- Prayer changes our attitudes about many things.
- Prayer helps us worship God on a deeper level.
- Prayer encourages us to pray from the Word of God.
- Prayer opens us to new vistas of ministry.

101

- Prayer encourages us to be open to receiving revelation and understanding of a passage of scripture.
- Prayer creates a desire to lean on Jesus rather than ourselves.

I am sure there are many more benefits and blessings, but I wanted to entice you with just a few, hoping you will have a hunger to learn more about the power of prayer. Prayer has not been an easy call for me.

When I was first involved in prayer times, I just listened to others pray. Maybe at some point I added a few words silently, but never, never did I dream that some day I would be called on to pray in front of many people, to be a leader in prayer, to chair two different prayer ministries, to write articles on prayer, or to spend so much time in prayer every day—even to mentor others in prayer. I have been asked to speak about prayer to groups of people. God dreams big dreams for us.

I have learned to *believe* God not just to believe *in* God, but to truly believe He is able to do all things. This has taken me a long time. There have been plenty of trials, mistakes, and hesitancy on my part to reach out for this along the way. But our God is faithful. He waits, always ready to give when we ask according to what His will is for us. When Jesus left us to be with the Father, He did not leave us unprepared to fight the enemy. We have the Holy Spirit sealed within us (2 Corin. 1:22). We have God's Word always available. We have the fellowship of other Christians in our church homes. We have the ability to come into the presence of the living God in our prayers and speak directly to Him. We have the gift of salvation in Christ Jesus by the grace of the almighty God. We can confess our sins and choose to repent (to turn away from the sin), thereby establishing a closer relationship to Jesus. We have such hope. Why am I mentioning this as a beginning to understanding more about prayer? Because we must understand that all prayer comes as a directive from God. He is always the instigator of prayer. We respond. We think we are the ones desiring to pray, but the Holy Spirit, who dwells in our hearts, is the One nudging us, whispering, "Turn to God, pray, ask, believe He is able." Awesome, isn't it?

One of the barriers to believing that I could pray aloud or in front of others was the feeling that my prayers would be simple. I had listened to many people whose prayers were beautiful, the words flowing eloquently, with passion and wisdom. Words tumbled from their lips when they quoted scripture or seemed to understand a situation more deeply than I thought possible. For some, their ability to lift up praise to God was absolutely beautiful. I felt so inferior in my abilities.

I would wait for others to pray and then quietly slip in a short sentence or sometimes even a phrase. Why do you think I felt this way? There is just one word to describe it—pride. And pride has no place in our relationship with Jesus. It took me a number of years to reach the point where I understood that my prayers came from the inspired knowledge of the Holy Spirit dwelling within me and not from my own wisdom. I learned that preaching to others during prayer was a definite turn-off. And, yes, occasionally I still hear people praying—actually it seems as though they are praying to the audience and not to God. I try to block out this type of prayer when I hear it and focus my thoughts on God. A few times I have been in a prayer group where this happens frequently. Whether it is actually a right or wrong way of praying is not for me to say. But since I feel uncomfortable in that kind of situation, I stop attending that kind of prayer group.

Another type of prayer I am uncomfortable with is that of prayer that gives God instructions. This type of prayer tells God when, why, and how to solve a situation. Since God knows all and sees all and has perfect wisdom and knowledge, why do we need to give Him instructions? To me, that is a way of saying to

God, "I don't think you can make the best decision in this situation. This is the way I want it done." Don't you imagine God laughs at that kind of prayer? After all, God sees the big picture, and we see a tiny segment of the situation. Actually, when we ask God to resolve a situation, the most important thing we can do is to give the situation to Him and trust He will know the best way to resolve it and believe that God loves the person and cares about the situation far more than we do.

Please remember, as I share these thoughts with you on prayer, I didn't know any of this or even understand a lot of what was happening as I started my journey of prayer. This is one of the reasons I wanted to include this chapter in my book. Perhaps I would have felt more at ease praying, would not have had as many doubts, or made as many mistakes, if I had been exposed to some guidelines at the beginning. As we seek the Lord in prayer more and more, our trust grows in His ability. And as our trust grows, God sees this and often blesses us with a specific gift for intercessory prayer. Some of these gifts are words of knowledge, discernment, wisdom, blessings, healing, rebuking, warfare, travailing, praying in tongues, interpretation of tongues, and prophetic. I want to explain these different gifts—as I understand them. When I first was exposed to different gifts I did not accept or understand and often was skeptical. The Lord taught me mostly by my observing, then questioning, then searching for answers and explanations. And at the right moment in His perfect planning, I have been given an ability to use most of the gifts mentioned above. Not all are ones that are constant in my daily praying. I never know when the Lord, through His Holy Spirit, will use me by one of the gifts I mentioned. Some people are given one or two very specific gifts and become quite well-known for the power released in those gifts. Others, like me, are given the gifts occasionally. I can tell you, each time it happens, I am completely overwhelmed that God would use me. It truly humbles me beyond words. And I thank my God over and over that He has chosen me to be a vessel to reach out and touch others to bring them closer to Him.

One of the gifts the Lord has given me is a word of knowledge. I can be praying with someone and a word will come into my mind that often is totally apart from what the prayer request is about. When that happens, I stop the prayer and say to the person, "I keep hearing a word that I don't understand. The word is _____." Sometimes before I can even ask, "Would you like me to pray about how this word (or phrase) applies to your situation?" the person responds that the words hit exactly on a deeper level of the problem. Often they thank me afterwards for touching that part of the situation. I always tell them I cannot take any credit for it because it is the Holy Spirit working through me to reach them and give them the assurance or comfort. And that is exactly what happens. We can never take credit for this kind of deep understanding or comprehension of more than was shared for prayer. If we do, surely we are opening ourselves up to the opportunity of being prideful and self-important. Then we cannot be used as God desires to use us. The same warning can be given for the gift of discernment or interpretation of what is said when someone speaks in tongues, or prophesizes. All these are gifts of the Spirit. And every one of these gifts is given to glorify our heavenly Father.

Actually, a very important part of my prayer every day is giving praise to God for how He uses me. I always thank Him and assure Him that the glory belongs to Him. I ask that He would always give me a heightened awareness of any leaning toward a prideful attitude in my praying for others.

Another gift given to me that has been ongoing is the gift of discernment when praying for others. When I first received this gift, I would pray aloud with someone and would hear a word or phrase in my mind. Often the word or phrase kept repeating in my mind. I didn't know what to do with it. So in my usual argumentative style, I would silently argue with God,

"Well, I can't say that out loud. What would the person think?"
"Yes, you can, trust Me." and this exchange would be argued
back and forth in my mind. Pride? Yep, it would rear its ugly
head quite often. The first time I finally said, "All right, I will
do this." to God, I remember taking a deep breath and saying
to the person, "I keep hearing a phrase over and over in my
mind. I am not sure what it means, but I want to tell you what
it is and perhaps it will mean something to you. Is that okay?"
The person said it was okay and I shared, and the person started
crying and said that was exactly what was bothering him or her
deep down inside. So then we prayed about that. If I had not
been obedient to the nudging of the Holy Spirit, perhaps the
part of the prayer that was so important for the person would
never have happened.

For years I was hesitant and almost always argued with the
Holy Spirit in my mind before venturing forth with the words.
It was silly of me, but that old pride just keeps rearing its ugly
head. I fight it all the time. Finally I began to feel more comfortable with receiving these words. Our God is so good. When
I trust Him, He never lets me down. Not once has a person
been offended. In fact, just the opposite is true. However, I
have schooled myself to realize there might come a time when
a person will reject the word of knowledge. If that happens, I
would say that it is okay, drop it, and go on with the prayer as
we had been before. It is always the choice of the person for
whom we are praying. Remember, we are servants called by God
to intercede in prayer for the person and not intended to be a
counselor to give answers or solutions. Knowing this gives us a
wonderful freedom in praying for others. I love knowing that
God is handling it, and I don't have to impress anyone with
having an answer or a solution.

After a few years I grew more comfortable with receiving
words of knowledge and the gift of discernment. The gift of

discernment gives me an understanding beyond my own wisdom to hear more than what a person says, and therefore I am able to pray more deeply for a specific situation. Not every time I pray are these gifts active. I never know when it will happen. But I have learned to be obedient in the use of these gifts. I always give God the glory. When a person thanks me for the insights, I always give the praise to the Holy Spirit. I tell people that God just uses me as a vessel through which His Holy Spirit is reaching out and touching that person. I cannot stress enough what freedom this gives us in praying for others. We don't have to have answers or solutions or to-do lists. Our role is to just lift that person and the situation up to the Lord. Then He takes over.

When we pray for others in the privacy of our homes, it is the same. We can listen for God to direct our prayers in ways we don't expect. We can weep for the person or situation, and we can pray for deliverance from the bondage of whatever is going on in the person's life. We can pray for people we don't even know, asking God's mercy, blessings, and compassion upon them. We can be standing in a check-out line and, instead of fretting over the wait, we can pray for the cashier or even the people in front of us. Of course, we are doing this silently. Actually, several times in a check-out line I have been doing this and when it is my turn, the cashier gives me a great big smile, a pleasant greeting. Hmmm?

Often I offer prayers to God on behalf of others when I drive. For some reason, when I pass a group of men working near or in a manhole, I pray for their safety. I don't know why; I just know I must do it. I always feel a sense of urgency about it as I pass them. So I just ask the Lord to protect them, to bless them, to help them know Jesus on a deep personal level. Then the feeling just goes away. I don't share this with you in order to brag but to encourage you to become bold in lifting up prayers even if you don't know why. Sometimes I think the Lord just wants us to be obedient to His guidance for us. He wants us to trust that when the Holy Spirit directs our thoughts we obey the directive. We don't have to know why or what the result is.

Perhaps you have heard someone tell about the people who pray and heat is generated from their hands. In the early stages of my prayer life, there were times when I would join hands with people and one person's hand would be so hot. I was told this is the flow of power from the Holy Spirit into and through the person God is using in prayer to touch the one being prayed for. The first time it happened to me, I was so excited. I felt so humbled to think God would use me in this way. I don't mention it to people or brag about it. Not every time I pray do I receive this wonderful gift. I don't say, "Today the heat from the Holy Spirit is going to pour through me." No, it is God's choosing. I am just so thankful to be used in the transference of the healing power of the Holy Spirit. Often when this happens tears pour forth from the person who is being prayed for. To me, this indicates the person has been touched by the power of the Spirit. It is a wonderful thing to see. Often, there is also a tingling. I find my prayers become more confident when this happens, probably because I am so aware of God's presence in the situation.

And do you know what else happens? Every time I have been involved in this type of wonderful prayer, it has drawn me closer to the Lord. I have become more trusting, more believing in God's power and ability and faith that nothing is too difficult for God. So praying for others as well as praying for self creates an atmosphere where the Holy Spirit can work in us to draw us closer to the Lord. Blessing upon blessing He bestows upon those who love and serve Him.

The gift of words of wisdom will often come as we pray for someone, and we give praise to God for the person. We will find ourselves saying something completely apart from the prayer request. It is always a builder-upper. It can actually happen during conversation about the prayer need. Once I was asked to pray with a man that was visiting our church. He lived in Alaska and was visiting family in Cincinnati. We prayed together, and then he asked me, "What did you mean when you prayed for my heart to be filled with Jesus and no longer be captive to the world's ways?" In my mind I was saying to myself, "I prayed that?" I have to share with you that over the years, unless I entered the thoughts in my journal, I do not remember what I have prayed. It seems God doesn't want me to have reason to recall the words and take any of the glory. So I prayed silently, "Spirit, help me." And out of my mouth came the words, "There is a freedom in following Jesus like nothing the world can ever give you." Later I shared this with Pastor Mike because it had seemed so special to me. Pastor Mike looked at me and said, "Where did that come from?" Then he shook his head and said "Of course, wisdom from the Spirit." Some time later I received a letter from that man after he was back in Alaska. He thanked me for the words given him and said they had opened up a new vista of his relationship with Jesus.

I shared with you about my mom and the healing of her eye problem. Deloros Winder has been given the marvelous gift of prayers of healing. Along with the healing gift are gifts of wisdom, discernment, and knowledge. They all work together to heal both physically and spiritually as God wills. There have been times when God has used me this way. But, again, not every time I pray. I believe when we pray for a person's healing we have to believe Jesus is the great healer. It is always asked for in His name. We have to believe the power generated from us is not our power but is the power of the Holy Spirit. We are simply the vessel the Lord is using at that moment. Praying this kind of prayer in a large group of people who are all coming forward for a type of healing is very draining. When I go home after this session of praying, I find the best thing for me to do is to sit quietly and let the Lord give me a fresh infilling of His

Spirit. How does this happen? I'm not sure. I just know that asking Him to fill me, to quiet my thoughts, to take away any desire to try and fix anything, to not take on any of the burden of pain, etc., energizes me and allows me to function without being overwhelmed with the burdens of others. God is so good.

Blessing prayers is a type of prayer that anyone can pray over another. We pray, giving thanks to God for the person's life, for the talents, the joy, or whatever we know about the person that is good. We ask the Lord to bless him or her or a family with all the spiritual blessings that God delights in bestowing upon his children. It has always been a special kind of praying that blesses me as well as the person I pray a blessing prayer for. It is such an uplifting type of prayer.

Rebuking prayer is the type of prayer that covers and protects a person or situation from being deceived or attacked by Satan. If you feel called to pray this type of prayer, I suggest you cover yourself with protection by asking the Lord's angels to form a hedge of protection round about you. As I mentioned in the chapter on Satan, he uses all kinds of deception to try and stop God's will from being done. This type of prayer is also very strenuous, and it is extremely important to stand on God's Word when praying a rebuking prayer.

Warfare praying is right up there with the rebuking prayers. Some people are drawn to praying for our cities, our country, our leaders, and the prevention of Satan's lies taking over. Warfare prayers (at least the ones I have been involved in) are usually very strongly spoken. Sometimes a person will feel led to walk around as he or she prays. This is a way to disturb the spirits of the air that might be trying to oppose the praying. This kind of praying takes boldness, believing God is able far beyond our capabilities, and an understanding of praying exactly what the Word of God states—the opposite of worldly ways.

Travailing prayer is a form of interceding for a person or situation where a person begins to feel overwhelmed with sorrow as he or she prays. The person begins to moan or groan as prayers are being lifted up. Tears might pour forth yet there is not crying like we ordinarily cry. Instead, it is weeping. This has happened to me periodically, always unexpectedly. I remember once recently as I was watching the national news. I wasn't even praying, and I saw a picture of lots of little children with looks of hunger. No place to reside seemed to be portrayed in that image. It grabbed at my heart, and I slid to my knees and started praying for all those little children. I was weeping and crying out to God for mercy and His compassion upon those innocent little ones. I don't know how long I prayed, but tears poured forth, and I could hear myself moaning. When God calls us to pray this way, it seems we pray for a specific time—the time God sets forth—and then we are released to go on about our business. I always sense a release in my spirit after this type praying—again to God's glory.

The gift of prophetic prayer is controversial I have found. For whatever reason, some people use this gift to exert control over a person or situation. I would think this does not please our God. The gift of prophetic is scriptural as many of the prophets and their prophecies are recorded in the Old Testament part of the Bible. I am not going to say much about this type of praying except that I do believe it is a gift God gives to certain people to be used very carefully. There are many excellent books in the Christian bookstores that can explain this gift better than I.

I have heard people quote the Bible about praying in secret and say we should therefore not pray in a group. From all my studies of Scripture I have come to the conclusion that surely the Lord is pleased when we pray together. Jesus taught the disciples when they asked how to pray, "Our Father...." (Matt. 6:9). This certainly would mean praying together, otherwise He would have said, "My Father..." Scripture also tells us "Again, I tell you that if two of you on earth agree about anything you ask for, it will be done for you by my Father in heaven. For where two or three come together in my name, there am I with them" (Matt. 18:19-20). When God is with us, surely there is much power released through His Holy Spirit. That is one of the most exciting things about praying together in a group—feeling the presence of the Holy Spirit. Sometimes waves of heat or a chill—like goose bumps—flow over me and tears fill my eyes and I simply bask in His presence. This happens often when a group has bonded together and is praying in agreement. I had to learn the meaning of "praying in agreement." It simply means that when one person in the group is praying aloud, the others agree with that person in their silent prayers. Perhaps one or more will audibly say, "Yes, Lord" or a quiet moaning sound will accompany the prayer being spoken. In other words, the prayer is actually being said by all, not just the one praying aloud. I believe this releases much power in the spiritual realms where there are constant battles between God's angels and the evil spirits.

When I pray in a group, we always begin our prayer time with reading scriptures and singing songs of praise to our Lord. We call on the name of Jesus, lifting praise to Him. Often we wave flags or banners and dance around the sanctuary. Then we finish with a song that expresses our worship as well as our praise of God. Many times the glory of the Lord seems to just fall on us. There is silence as we kneel at the front of the sanctuary, or often a person lies prostrate on the floor. Sometimes there is weeping or a soft intoning of heavenly language (speaking in tongues).

All of it is beautiful, very moving, and takes us completely out of self into a focus totally on the Lord. Then we are ready to pray—trusting we are praying the desires of God's heart. This is another area that I seem to have fallen into, that of being a leader in the praise and worship time. I have many cassette tapes and CDs that I use from which I pick out three or four songs to sing each time we meet. I always ask the Holy Spirit to guide me as I spread all the song sheets out on the floor. It is continually amazing to me how the music and scriptures fit right along with the prayer concerns the others bring to the meeting. The scriptures that I am guided to choose often become part of our prayers throughout our time together. I truly enjoy doing this planning part of the prayer meeting. Never did I dream in the beginning of my search for God that I would be involved in this type of prayer and worship. What a joy I experience in the Lord using me in this way!

Another part of prayer that I did not understand for quite some time is praying in tongues. When these unusual sounds started coming from my lips I hardly knew what to do. I didn't understand. I certainly did not want to speak them in front of anyone else. I did not even tell people that I was given this gift at first. However, over the years I have come to enjoy this gift very much. I call it "my heavenly language." This type of praying is not the kind that is prophetic and requires interpretation from others. This praying of heavenly language reaches deeper into focusing my thoughts on the Lord—my desire to praise Him more deeply, to draw closer to Him, to express beyond the English language the very wonderful, awesome, greatness of who He is. We can do this with our heavenly language. When I first heard people praying like this, I thought how beautiful, but how do they have the nerve to speak in a funny language? I then began to notice that every single person spoke with a different sound or dialect or inflection. When I pray in the heavenly language I feel so close to God. I feel so humble, so overwhelmed with love and a sense of wonderful peace and joy and reverence.

Some people ask for this gift. I have been in prayer groups where we have prayed with a person to receive this gift from the Holy Spirit, and I have seen the prayers answered; and, yes, not answered. I do not believe you have to pray in tongues in order to be filled with the Holy Spirit. I have found nothing in Scripture that says this is a requirement. However, I do believe that when we give over control of ourselves, stop worrying so much about how others perceive us when we pray, and focus our prayers directly on God, we become more open to receiving this precious gift. I know people who are deeply committed Christians, who love the Lord, who serve him faithfully, and yet do not have this particular gift. Does that mean the person is not filled with the Spirit, as some say? I don't think so.

Why must we label people? Why do we feel we must prove our spirituality? Again, I believe this is a type of pride and not what God desires for us. One of the things I sense helps us to be open to receiving this gift is a person's ability to pray out loud, by themselves as well as with others. Heavenly language is a type of singing, kind of a humming or chanting, and needs to be audible in order to flow into the spiritual realms and dispel evil spirits. I also believe that when we pray in our heavenly language together, such power is released because of our praising God in a language He gives us. Surely this is one explanation for what scripture says, "In the same way, the Spirit helps us in our weakness. We do not know what we ought to pray for, but the Spirit himself intercedes for us with groans, that words cannot express" (Rom. 8:26). Of course, this scripture also tells us the Holy Spirit will guide us in our prayer life if we ask and help us formulate our prayer requests to conform to what God's will for the situation is.

What else can I say about this gift of heavenly language? One thing I have not seen mentioned about praying in tongues, at least in the books I have read, is the fact we can control whether or not we pray in tongues. It is a gift we choose to use or not use. It is a gift that I believe should only be used in a situation where others would feel comfortable hearing it. When we pray individually with a person and the desire to pray in tongues arises, I would stop and ask the person if it would be all right to do that. Otherwise the praying in tongues can come across as an attitude of superiority or heightened spirituality, and that is the last thing I believe the Lord would want us to have the other person focused on when we pray for him or her. Praying in tongues is a marvelous way of praising God, of expressing joy in His awesome wonderfulness. It is a way of expressing deep, inner reverence of the Lord. It is not a tool to impress others. It is not something to feel smug about. When I lead a prayer group, occasionally I sense an urgent need for us to pray in tongues. But before I begin, I always announce to the group that I would like us to do this only if they feel led to do so. Then there is the freedom to respond individually as the Holy Spirit leads them. The praying in tongues might last a minute or perhaps two, sometimes longer. It seems when the urgency is over the sounds fade softly. Then there is quiet, a poignant silence before we start our regular praying again. Beautiful. Usually everyone is praying at the same time. So what you hear is a delightful joining of sounds that harmonize. It astounds me. I can't really explain it more than this, but I am thankful to have received this gift. I see nothing wrong with asking for this gift, but please never feel you are less than another as a prayer warrior or intercessor simply because you do not pray in tongues.

Pride is the worst enemy of committed prayer. When we pray, to whom are we praying—the people around us, the individual who perhaps asked for prayer? Neither. We are praying to the Lord, asking Him to intervene, to solve a situation, to open doors or close them, according to His great wisdom. Do you think God cares that every word we speak is perfect? Or that we must have a terrific claim to good grammar? Does God care if we repeat ourselves? What if we stumble over a sentence and it becomes a fragment that is not clear to others? What happens if we pause to gather our thoughts and perhaps stutter a word or two? My answer to all of these questions is—God only wants our sincere hearts, our willingness to put others before ourselves, to trust He can answer and solve all our problems, to trust He is God! If the person for whom we are praying—or if we are in a prayer group and others are focusing on the way we pray rather than the words spoken from our hearts—then those persons are not focusing on God, and that is sad. Remember, we are imperfect, yet God desires to use us. He treasures our prayers so much that they are poured into bowls, as of incense, and offered up before Him by angels (Rev. 8:3-4). The first time I read that in Revelation and realized how much God desires our prayers and how He treasures them, it changed my whole attitude about praying. I pray because God calls me to do this. If He calls me to pray, He calls you to pray. There is no room for pride that we are doing a good thing for God. On the contrary, He is doing a good thing for us. He is creating in us a desire to do His will. Awesome, isn't it, when we start to realize how much God desires us to be centered on Him, as imperfect as we are.

I have often heard people praying with hesitancy in their voices or words when asking God's intervention. The prayers often end with, "if it is your will Lord." It is so important that when we pray we trust that God is able to do all things. When we ask for His intervention, then we should believe what we are asking is possible for Him to do. Remember, Scripture tells us that nothing is impossible for God. Do we trust that God is able? Do we trust that God can make the best decision? Or do we think we know better than God how to handle and proceed with a request? If our first two answers are yes and the third is no, we are well on the way to a positive, assured type of praying. When we pray with hesitancy, no doubt the person we are praying for will sense this and not feel God can do what we are asking. Our trust in the power of prayer goes a long way toward giving confidence and assurance to the person requesting prayer. This is so important.

Often when a person asks for a specific answer or result, I pray that God would open the right doors and close those doors that would not be pleasing to Him. I usually ask for God's angels to be around the person as the answer comes, to protect and guide and comfort. Actually praying with trust in God frees us from having to try to figure out the best way for a solution to a problem. It was a wonderful eye-opener to me when I finally realized that God always sees the bigger picture. What I would like to see resolved for the moment might, in the end, not be the best. Since our God has perfect wisdom and all knowledge, He can see the big picture and perhaps the prayer will be answered in a different way than we expected. Or it might take much longer than we hoped. Nevertheless, I truly believe God hears, acts, and answers prayers.

One last area of prayer I want to mention is the one of worship styles in prayer meetings. When I first started attending conferences and observing freedom in worship, I felt somewhat uncomfortable. The lifting of hands during singing always fascinated me. Why would people want to do that? I saw them sway with the music and lift their hands high above their heads. Often their eyes were closed. One time I happened to look down at my hands. They were tightly grabbing the back of the pew in front of me. Was I resisting something the Holy Spirit wanted me to enjoy? It wasn't until 1995 that I began to have enough courage to lift my hands—just a little—as we sang worship songs. But, oh, what a feeling of drawing closer to the Lord it gave me!

In certain prayer groups or contemporary worship services or worshipping at home, alone, I so enjoy the freedom of lifting my hands, swaying with the music, and waving banners, and even beyond that, dancing in place with praises to God pouring forth in song. Oh, what a blessing! What a joy! What a wonderful sense of being open to hearing God's voice, to being reassured of His great love! Even as I write this, I think about how reserved I used to be and how I judged those who enjoyed this type of worship. As usual, God was teaching me a lesson. We can worship and pray to our God in a quiet way. We can do it in a more exuberant way. We can do it in between these two styles. All are good. One is not better than another. I believe the important thing is to reach out, try a new way. Find where God wants us to be in worship and prayer with Him. Above all, we should not judge others for the way they worship. Again, at least for me, there has been a deep longing fulfilled in my heart as I have learned to express myself more openly. God just keeps doing new things with me. I have been on a continual learning curve ever since those long ago words were uttered by the retired minister, "God is growing you." To be honest, it has now become an eagerness or anticipation for what God will do next in me. I constantly thank Him for using me and teaching so much and for His constant blessings in my life.

Would I want to trade places with the person I was back in 1979? Well, in age, yes. But in growing closer to God? No. I was so lost. I was so fearful. Prayer has become a lifeline for me. I have often said, "It is as necessary to me as breathing." May you, too, know that wonderful fulfillment as God grows you in your prayer life and your service to the Lord.

CHAPTER 9

I have been sharing with you the joy of praying and also the fact that God has me on a continual learning curve. Another new thing was the area of teaching. I mentioned earlier that I had started attending adult Sunday school classes, thinking it would help me understand what was going on in my life. I attended faithfully all through the 1980s, but in the fall of 1990 I joined a class that offered a really deep study of the Bible. We had to memorize 60 verses over the two year course. I believe this started my love affair with Scripture. As a result of that class, I took training to teach this in-depth Bible study. This began another new area to which God called me. I never dreamed I would be a teacher of the Bible for other adults. For two more years I led this intense Bible study. Later, I taught it again for another two years. I continue to teach and lead studies. How I enjoy it! There is nothing as thrilling as seeing a person's face light up with understanding or a revelation of Scripture. I have learned to research a specific topic and then write a paper about it as a handout during class study. For many years I asked Pastor Mike to review the prepared handout first to be sure it was theologically correct, for I want to be a teacher who teaches only the truth as Scripture states it. The advice Pastor Mike gave me so long ago holds true continually in my teaching "You don't have to know all the answers." I always tell a new class this at the outset of our study. I do promise, to the best of my ability, to find an answer for them. The unique thing about this is that I always learn so much myself. Teaching others, in my estimation, is a continual learning process for the teacher. There is always a new way of leading a person to understanding, a new approach or opinion to be received from the people in the group.

I always pray before each lesson and ask the Holy Spirit to speak through me. I ask that the Spirit will give revelation to the group and, as a result, they will be drawn closer to our Lord. God has been so good in blessing our studies. We share, we laugh, we tease, we weep, we memorize Scripture, and we bond as brothers and sisters in Christ Jesus. What a wonderful gift God blessed me with in giving me the opportunity to teach what the Holy Spirit has been showing me for such a long time. There will never be enough time to teach on all the wonderful books and scriptures available to us.

God's timing in opening this door for me was a lot longer than I would have planned—naturally. You no doubt are aware by this time that I tend to zip right into something without thinking about the obstacles. God knew, however, I needed much time to absorb His truths and to reach the point where I truly believed what I was saying and teaching. I needed to reach a point where what I was teaching would be accepted by others because they could see the joy and excitement in me.

Another spin-off from the teaching was writing articles about prayer for the church newsletter. It is fun each month to ask the Holy Spirit what scripture to use—and He graciously guides me. Then I simply start writing how I feel about the scripture, drawing upon my experiences and often quoting from someone else's excellent thoughts. I cannot tell you how many times people have called me or written me a note or stopped me in various places at church to express how much these articles meant to them. People have told me they cut out the articles and carry them in their purses or put them on their bedside tables or save all of them for future reference or fasten them on their refrigerators. One person mails them to a friend. Some have said I must have written the article just for them. I cannot take credit for the content of the articles. I truly believe the credit must go to the Holy Spirit. It is the same with this book. I write a chapter, pick it up a few weeks later, and know exactly what should be changed. Sometimes I am cleaning the house or driving the car and an idea just pops into my mind. I have learned to jump up and write the ideas down when they come as I am reading fiction or watching TV. I have no control over these thoughts. They just come. God is so very good. How could I think otherwise? He keeps giving me the opportunity to use ordinary talents in extraordinary ways.

I would love to have the opportunity to teach about prayer at other churches. Perhaps some day this will happen. I have never actively sought any of the opportunities that have come my way. I believe each one has been orchestrated by the Holy Spirit. I am learning to allow God to fulfill His plan for my life more as I grow in understanding of His awesome abilities. It is never easy. I always have excuses or a reason why I cannot do a particular thing. Then I take a second to think, *What am I doing? I am not trusting that God is able.* I have been assured that when I am serving the Lord in whatever capacity He places me, the Spirit will guide me, protect me, and give me wisdom beyond my own. This belief helps me take the step into the uncharted waters I referred to in the beginning of this book.

I encourage you to participate in a study of God's Word. Once you start—and if you have a dedicated teacher—you will find a continual hunger to study more and more. The scriptures will speak to needs or questions you might have. The truth of God's Word, the ultimate destiny of Jesus, the gift of the Holy

Spirit, the revelation of what is to come—all these things will become much clearer. Arguments contrary to the Word simply go away. And the expression I have heard so many times and wondered about, "I know that I know that I know" has become part of my vocabulary because I know that everything I have learned from study of the Word is true. So I know that what I now know is true. There is no doubt that the most wonderful part of all this is knowing that I will constantly understand and know more about God's truth as I continue to study. It is a never ending challenge and delight.

From the study of the Word I have begun to understand what it means when a believer says, "God has called you to…" I used to think, *How would I know? What is my call? Isn't it just enough to accept Jesus as Lord and Savior? Why is it important? What does it mean to be called?* I hope some of these questions have been answered for you—they have for me—as I share what has happened in my spiritual life which, by the way, spills over into every part of my worldly life.

God's call on my life is for me to fulfill the purpose or plan He had for me when I was created. No, it is not enough to just accept Jesus. Because once we do, if we do not grow in understanding, we miss out on the daily joy of serving our Lord. It is important because first the Lord loves us. Our understanding and accepting that should create a desire in us to respond with a love that wants to give; in other words, a desire to serve Him. A call from the Lord may be something as simple as being an usher at Sunday morning services, a greeter at the church door, someone who bakes sweets for the lonely or sick or elderly. It can be sending notes to shut-ins or being an encourager to someone who is having trouble. The list goes on and on. We aren't all called to be in the limelight, or become known as great leaders. God calls some to those positions, and it is wonderful. However, I do believe that the bigger the call, the more accountability is required to always give God the glory, and leaders will be tempted by the evil one more openly. Please never diminish the call God has on your life. We might never know in this life how we have touched others, but God knows. And after all, when we are serving the almighty God, the very best thing we can hear, are words whispered silently in our hearts, "Well done, good and faithful servant."

There is one more phrase I heard so much and wondered about at the beginning of my journey. That is, "Is this God's will for you?" My question was, "How do I know what God's will for me is? What does this mean? How do I know I am doing God's will? I asked one of the leaders in our church about this. He told me to start reading the Word and it would be revealed to me. Great! That was not the answer I wanted to hear. More study. I often felt like a big sponge, soaking up all this great information, but I received it so quickly that I couldn't retain it all.

However, since I was told to research the question in God's Word, I started doing that. The answer did not come quickly. It took several years. I believe God's will for me is described throughout this book. Little steps of faith, one on top of the other. God's will was "growing me." I share more about understanding God's will in chapter 13.

I hope to teach as long as God wants to use me. Of course, there will come a time when my thoughts won't be as sharp or my energy level will drain more quickly. But I don't worry about tomorrow. One of the very special gifts God has poured on me has been acceptance and the ability to savor the moment. What I did yesterday is over with, finished. What comes tomorrow, I leave to the Lord to help me through, but today—today, I can savor. Today I can use the time to learn more about the Lord, His goodness, His Holy Spirit, His plan for me. Today, I can enjoy the fun opportunities of being with friends or family or doing ministry work or reading, playing bridge, or golfing. If I am having a rough day, (and I do have them), I can pray for God to help me through it. Today, I can play uplifting Christian music to fill my home with reminders of His goodness. God's blessings—they are truly wonderful. I am sure they are different for each of us. We just need to look for them, to have awareness beyond normal chores, TV, and concerns. God has promised He will see us through any trouble and strengthen us by His might, and then we can rejoice in His goodness. He loves us so.

CHAPTER 10

Experiences from Christian Conferences

In the summer of 1992, Elaine, Pastor Mike's wife, asked me if I would be interested in attending a convention in Arlington, Virginia, put on by "Women of Faith." I said I would, not even knowing exactly what it was all about but figuring it would be a good experience for me. That's another example of my impulsive nature, just leaping into something without weighing the outcome. As I have read over the experiences I am sharing in this book, I realize God uses my impulsive nature to take me into new understandings of His call on my life. Perhaps I would have said no if I knew beforehand what was going to happen, especially in areas where I had doubt.

My good Christian friend Bettilee Perkins was to be my roomie. As usual, I had no idea this was going to be used by God to teach me so much. The conference was called "Prayer Gathering on the Potomac '92," September 11-13, 1992.

As I prayed about attending this gathering, I asked the Lord what I should be looking for. The inner voice of my spirit encouraged me to be sensitive to everything around me, to look at faces, watch expressions, take notes about my feelings of the moment, note whatever jumped out at me from the speakers.

So I was prepared with an outline of how I should participate. Was I ever in for a surprise!

A little history about the organization might be helpful to understand what I experienced. This was their first national prayer gathering. The group believed there were three things that must be done:

1. Be a force in the place of prayer to affect our nation.
2. Be godly examples of womanhood.
3. Take whatever political or social action that God would have them take in His behalf regarding the issue of child abuse/pornography, which they felt had become so evident in our nation. They believed this should be brought to light for those who intercede in prayer to God. The intercessors would be made aware of how this issue damages lives.

I am going to tell you exactly how I perceived things from my notes of so many years ago. Do you think God encouraged me to journal my thoughts in 1992 knowing I would be writing about the event all these years later? I will not use real names for the testimonies I relate. I have either changed the names or omitted the name because I believe the importance of the telling is not who the person is but what the person has been through and how God touched his or her life and changed it.

We arrived on Friday morning, checked in, and then decided to have lunch—eating is a big thing at conferences. We met up with another church friend, Patty, and found a table. Patty noticed a woman sitting by herself at another table and asked her to join us. During our discussions, this woman shared that she had been molested as a child. She is a spirit-filled person from California, apparently quite active in doing what she can to fight pornography. She shared having been on a popular TV show in debate about pornography with an ACLU (American

Civil Liberties Union) lawyer. She told how very aware God has made her by signs that He was with her in serving Him. On the way to the TV show the driver of the limo that was taking her through the rush hour traffic said, "In twenty years this has never happened, no traffic in front, no traffic in back, the way is clear." She had been very nervous about whether this was right to do and believed this was a sign to her that God approved, and she thanked Him for the sign. She was quite a talker—very free in her praise to the Lord, almost as if God was her best friend and advisor and everyone should know that God was the cause of everything good that happened in her life. She came across to me as sincere, bold, outgoing, eager, and confident—and I wrote these thoughts down immediately after lunch. Later I was told this woman had been sexually abused by several foster fathers in the homes where she had been placed as a girl. At the end of the Prayer Gathering we met her in the lobby. She told us that God had made her whole. However she gets weary at times with all the sadness she is exposed to by ones who seek her out for comfort. Yet she cannot stop because she believes this is what God is calling her to do.

Stop–fast forward to the present. Just this first incident shows how God guides us when we faithfully desire to serve Him and try to be obedient to His guidance. Many times God takes awful things done to us by the evil in the world and turns them around for good, such as this woman who has comforted and counseled so many other women who had been in similar circumstances. People's free will can cause us pain, but God can bring us through the pain and make us whole through the love of Christ Jesus when we turn to Him, trust Him and believe in Him. Being able to share what God has done in our lives through difficult situations often helps the person grow in their understanding of God's love for us–and most of the time the one sharing will never know how the listener was touched. I call it "spreading the seeds of faith for our dear Lord to be nurtured by His Holy Spirit." And who are the gardeners? Us–as we are guided by the Holy Spirit to respond to the need we see or feel in God's hurting people, nurturing them, just as we tend a garden.

Now back to 1992. We went into the meeting area. I looked around at the faces of the hundreds of women, all ages and many nationalities. The main thing I noticed was the lack of a keep-your-distance attitude. Many had smiles on their faces. There were friendly exchanges; all over the area, voices could be heard murmuring praise to our Lord or thanking Him as they talked within their groups. This was just awesome to me. Especially when I remembered all the years I kept my distance, avoiding sharing too much with others.

During the afternoon and evening there were several great speakers, lots of worship music, and special soloists. There were testimonies from some of the speakers that would bring tears to my eyes. At one point the regular program was stopped and it was announced that a hurricane, force four, was expected to hit Oahu between 4:00 and 9:00 P.M. that day. One woman led all of us in prayer to ask God to avert the hurricane and to save the people and the city. The room was filled with the women praying aloud. There were sounds of moaning and people praying in tongues. All of a sudden, my heart felt filled with overwhelming sorrow and anguish. My eyes filled with tears. I could sense a power being unleashed all around me, surely the power of God.

We then prayed that our presence be lifted to Jesus, that we would be holy and acceptable for Him to do His will through us and in us. Then a man, one of the guest speakers, started praying that Jesus would walk the streets that very night and convict men who were searching for pornography. He prayed Jesus would help them turn away, defeat Satan, as God had helped him turn from pornography and become a new person in Christ Jesus. It was so very moving. As I was praying this in agreement silently, the murmuring of the crowd became stronger and stronger. My heart again felt overwhelmed. I could sense the grieving of the Holy Spirit for all these men. I could hardly stand it. I wanted to weep for the grief these men were probably causing family, friends, and themselves.

As we were all praying, the language of tongues became louder and louder, and in my inner spirit it came to me, "Do you hear this? These are my prayer warriors. Each of them is praying out of conviction, out of love, hear them, listen." Then we joined hands with the persons on either side of us. The woman on my left was praying softly in tongues and all of a sudden I just knew some of the things she was saying. At first I thought, *How could I possibly know what she is saying?* Then I thought, *Well, it must be the Holy Spirit. Should I share this with her?* Then I remembered what had been taught to me about being bold in the Spirit. During the break time, hesitantly I asked her if she wanted to know what I believed she had been praying. She gave permission and I shared the words I had heard, but I could not remember the last phrase. She thanked me anyway and as I sat back down and wrote the words I had shared with the woman—at that very moment the rest of the interpretation became immediately clear. "Lord I am praying for the lost, for the unloved, for those who are not convicted." At the close of the session I said to her that I knew what the rest of the words were. Did she want to hear? Again she eagerly agreed, so I shared that the words were "for those not convicted." She looked at me and said, "Praise the Lord. I have been praying for my father to be convicted. God is so good."

Reader, think about what had just happened. This was such a perfect example of understanding about praying in tongues. The woman was being faithful in praying in the heavenly language and crying out for her father's conviction. By God giving me the interpretation, He was affirming her faithfulness in praying for her father. For my part I was being obedient—scared, hesitant—but obedient. This did nothing for my glory, but showed God's love and assurance to this woman that God heard her prayer. He was comforting her through another's voice and words. You must remember this was all very new to me. I was nervous, elated, excited, awed, and this was only the first day.

During the afternoon one of the prayer leaders told us she was led to read Jeremiah 9:17-21, which included saying women were being called to travailing prayer. She felt it prophetic for that time. She also said we were in a war for the soul of our nation—and as the years have gone by, I believe her words were prophetic indeed.

After the break and dinner we were back in the conference room. Several women shared about homosexuality, sexual molestation, and abuse. There were times of prayer regarding these issues, and the women were lamenting and wailing and moaning in unison prayers, seeking God's mercy and help. There was such a feeling of power in the praying, such a feeling of humility, of knowing that God grieves daily—continually—for His people who make the choice to walk in darkness. I had never heard this type praying before, although I had read about it in Scripture. This was before I started a prayer group where we also prayed frequently in this way. Again, the Lord was teaching me and preparing me. The sound is almost musical. Individual voices are not heard, just a unison sound that flows upward and outward, softly, then louder, then softly again and eventually just fades into a poignant silence.

Perhaps this type praying is not comfortable for everyone; however, it is beautiful and I could find nothing unscriptural about it. In fact, by the time we returned to our room, I was emotionally exhausted. There was so much to absorb and so many new experiences. I knew it would take time to sink in. It was a wonderful day. My friend turned on the news to see what the weather was like in Hawaii. The hurricane had been diverted from the island of Oahu.

The next morning one of the soloists sang "I Am." Oh, the power of her voice—the adulation she seemed to be giving to God as she sang! It seemed as if she was lifting the women up to God. There were shouts of joy, clapping, tears, and smiles. And then I heard in my inner spirit the words; "When a person sings to Me, when that person sings to worship God, and not for performance, then I give that person the voice of an angel. At that moment the person is anointed. That person is My gift to My children for that moment to stir their hearts, to bring them closer to Me." Is that not beautiful? Doesn't this show how our Lord cares about even the details of our worship of Him?

Angels—how often they were referred to during this conference. I asked myself, *Is it only those who have a very deep relationship with God who understand and acknowledge God's angels?* At times there was mention of God's warring angels, His ministering angels, His protecting angels, always at His call in our midst, whether we see them or sense them. Later, as we were singing "Onward Christian Soldiers," I noticed that angels were mentioned in the song. I felt there was something I would understand in a new way regarding God's angels and their purpose in God's scheme of things by the time the conference was over. During the Saturday evening session another soloist, this time a man, mentioned angels. He said the heart of the angel is holy and pure. What a beautiful thought.

Throughout each session of the conference there was much time for corporate prayer. I found myself praying more earnestly than I had ever prayed before. On Saturday afternoon we broke into groups and walked around the grounds of the capitol and prayed over Washington D.C. We could choose the area where we would pray so I chose the Lincoln Memorial—because I was born on Lincoln's birthday. Good reason, right? I was so new at this and so completely unaware of how my worldly reasons for doing things were being battered down and how the Holy Spirit was showing me a new way of thinking. Our group was led by a very spirited intercessor who had a ministry for street people in the area. Her name was the same as mine, Evelyn. As we were walking through the park area where the Vietnam Memorial is, my heart started getting heavier and heavier. I felt short of breath. I wanted to just stop and cry. Finally, I asked Evelyn, "What in the world is happening to me? Should I stop and go back to the hotel?" She just smiled and said, "God is giving you a deep understanding of the grieving of the ones who gave their lives in Vietnam and for those veterans who are standing here in these little stalls whose lives seem lost. God wants them to be found and is calling you to just pray for them as you walk." Well, that was definitely a new thing to me. Yet I believed she knew what she was talking about. So I did as she suggested and prayed all the way through the park. Interestingly, as I would pass a stall, the man behind the table would often look directly into my eyes. I smiled and prayed each time, "God, please touch him. May he not be lost to you." As we left the park, all the feelings I expressed above just disappeared. God's Holy Spirit was teaching me another new thing.

Another thing I noticed was that I could not eat. It seemed I was so emotionally charged with a heightened awareness of all that was happening around me that there was no hunger for ordinary food. I tried eating a pretzel, but it stuck in my throat. I could only eat a little at dinner. That evening during one of the sessions I thought, "I am not the same woman that came here on Friday. The Lord has reached out through His Holy Spirit and changed me, taught me, made me aware of how His power is released through prayer." And God wasn't through with me yet.

On Sunday morning Bettilee and I got up bright and early to attend a morning worship service. The music was soft, gentle, but penetrating. The words of the songs seemed to settle deep into my thoughts. There was a talk on addictions, and prayers were offered regarding the sin of pornography. Prayers were offered for many of the leaders of the seminar. Then, in my heart, I heard the words, "Here is the change that I promised you. It will be hard. You promised me you were ready. I will strengthen you. I will speak through you. Be obedient to Me, for I have called you to serve; to be my spokesman for prayer in your area. Remember the glory is Mine." I quickly wrote all this down, actually not really comprehending the depth of meaning at that moment. I was caught up in the next beautiful part of the morning. Kay Williams, the leader of a ministry of the American Christian Trust Standards of Praise, was speaking about banners being a part of worship. She explained that while the function of banners is to unite people, sometimes it can divide them. Visual items will do one or the other. Banners presented to the glory of our Lord move through the air and disperse evil spirits. The banners take up room the evil spirits might try to occupy. This was another new thought for me.

The procession of banners started. The music was strong and powerful, yet almost danceable. The banners were huge and each one was carried by a man. As the banners were presented in the procession, each representing one of the twelve tribes of Israel, my thoughts came quickly, and my feelings seemed to be in tune with the glorious, moving, and swaying of the banners. The jewels sparkled like diamonds. The colors were vibrant, strong, and powerful. The music was a chant from olden times. The bells fastened on the banners tinkled, ringing softly as the banners passed by my area. The pictures sewn into the huge silken cloths—the sun, sword, treasure chest, doe, donkey, a tree, lion, a house, the wheat, flowers, a menorah, a ship—reflected a brilliance that was almost indescribable. There was silence in the room full of people. There was a feeling of awe, of reverence, of the presence of God. And then my friend whispered, "Look behind you Evelyn."

There was the most beautiful banner of silver and deep blue and gold representing the Lamb of God, Jesus. A man was holding the huge banner and just standing at the back of the center aisle. The glistening of the cloth, the soft breeze moving the banner, the Holy Spirit impressing the moment on my heart; I simply could not stand there. I had to fall on my knees in humility and in thanks and praise to my Lord. You have to understand that this was not a common occurrence for me to so openly demonstrate emotions from deep inside me. As I got up, hastily I jotted down my thoughts and later formulated them into this prose.

"Arise–Shine"

The procession of banners
How glorious, how moving
How exalted it makes one feel
That we are in touch with the God of all time.
The jewels sparkle like diamonds,
The colors, vibrant, strong, powerful.
The music, a chant from olden times.
The bells tinkle,
Ringing softly in the procession.
The sparkling threads of color
Creating the emblems of the twelve tribes of Israel.
The sun, the sword, the tents, the doe,
The donkey, the ship, the lion, the wolf,
The brilliance is almost indescribable.
The silence of the worshippers
The feeling of awe, reverence.
The presence of God is seemingly felt all around.
And then, the banner of all banners,
The Lamb of God representing Jesus.

The colors, blue and gold and silver, glistening in the
    light,
The soft breeze moving the folds of the banner,
The Holy Spirit impressing the moment on my heart.
I could hear sobs around me, indrawn breaths,
As if people were overwhelmed with the beauty
The poignancy of the moment.
I could not stand there
I fell to my knees in humbleness and thankfulness,
In praises to Jesus, praises to God, the Almighty, the
    Most High.

Written September 13, 1992

Even now, many years later, as I write this from my notes
of l992, it brings tears of joy to my eyes and a sense of refresh-
ment to my soul. Bettilee and I were so moved at the end of this
time we simply got up and left before the business part of the
meeting resumed. It was a time when we simply did not want
to talk or to think about anything worldly. It was time to just
be and to allow the Holy Spirit to help process what we had
experienced. We went back to our room, climbed on the beds,
prayed, and shared with each other what we had just witnessed.
This weekend together cemented our friendship into one that
has been lasting and joyful to this very day.

Upon our return to Cincinnati, Pastor Mike asked us to
give a short report of our experiences during the following Sunday morning service. It wasn't easy to wrap up in a few short
sentences the magnitude of the transformation that had taken
place in my heart and mind that weekend. It truly began a new
direction for the ministry I was called to.

Several weeks later during our Sunday morning church service, the thought came how wonderful it would be to have the
banner ministry come to our town so people could experience
what I had experienced. Of course, I did not realize then that

not everyone experiences the same thing or is affected to the same degree during a shared meeting or conference or worship time. I was eager to bring the banner ministry to our church. How would this idea come to pass?

While I was at the conference I had purchased five books I thought might be of interest in pursuing a better understanding of prayer and ministry of prayer. But after arriving home, working full time, and spending time with family, I had not even glanced at any of them. In fact, I had piled them on my desk and forgotten about them. During this time I also had three separate occasions when a person said I should read the book, *Possessing The Gates of the Enemy* by Cindy Jacobs, the co-founder and president of Generals of Intercession, an international prayer ministry that helps build prayer movements throughout the world. I wasn't sure about all this praying against the evil spirits, even though I had witnessed quite a bit of it at the seminar in Washington, D.C. After so many suggestions that I should read this book I figured it must be something God wanted me to read. The next Saturday I decided to clean off my desk. When I picked up the pile of books I had bought at the conference there was the book by Cindy Jacobs. I had forgotten I had even purchased it. Do you think there was a message here for me? So I read it. I was impressed by the sincerity of Cindy Jacob's experiences and her clearly stated suggestions of what is right and what isn't when it comes to praying against the enemy and for God.

Oh, how God works his plans in us! I casually mentioned to one of my friends at church, who was the first to suggest I read the book, how much I liked it and how impressed I was with Cindy Jacobs. My friend said, "We should have a conference and invite her to be the speaker. Why don't you check it out?" I thought, *Oh, why not! Duh!* Simple words to begin another life-changing experience.

So I wrote a letter to Cindy Jacobs asking her if she would consider coming to Cincinnati to speak on prayer—or on whatever subject she felt God's leading. After several months it was planned she would come to Cincinnati in 1994. Cindy Jacobs expressed that in her prayers for direction it had been shown to her that Cincinnati would be a key city in revival and reconciliation.

Then the idea of having the Acts of Praise (the banner ministry) to be part of the seminar sounded good. I contacted Kay Williams and Cindy Jacobs to see whether they were both in agreement these two events could work together. So the conference plans were born. I have to tell you, I had no idea what was entailed in putting together a city-wide conference. Actually, in the beginning I just thought it would be a nice thing to do. Little did I know. I started pulling a team together to work with me. Women from four different churches with different worship styles and traditions agreed to be part of this. As we met to plan all the details, we prayed and prayed for God to direct how it should be done. One of the gals and I started visiting churches of varying denominations, explaining to the pastors what we were going to be offering and why. The *why* had come to us that this was a way for our city to be united as one body in prayer and praising our God, regardless of where we attended church on Sunday mornings and regardless of the color of our skin or the culture in which we lived. Almost all the pastors were gracious and enjoyed sharing with us concerns of their respective churches. We would ask permission to stop in their sanctuaries before leaving, and we would pray God's blessing upon that church and upon the body of believers. From this particular part of the planning I came to realize how burdened most pastors are. I sensed exhaustion, discouragement, their feelings of not always having enough support from their congregations to carry out programs and to minister to the body, the extreme demands on their time. I derived from this that the enemy constantly battles against the needed serenity of pastors services when they are called by God to serve and lead the people.

Out of this part of planning, the input of the six gals on the planning team, the input of others that we talked to, and input from Cindy Jacobs, a dream was formed:

- This event will be the catalyst for churches to come together in a united interest for our city and to pray together for Cincinnati to be a light on the hill, reflecting the love of Jesus Christ.
- From this event we hope the body of Christ can truly get beyond individual differences, accepting each other as we are, and then be in unity in our likeness–that is the Lordship of Jesus.

I found this so exciting I could hardly wait for each new morning. I discovered prayer groups were springing up around the city, praying for the city and for revival to come here and for racial reconciliation. I was informed that several well-known Christian speakers were coming to area churches and giving prophecies that God was going to use this city in revival and reconciliation. One of the groups forming in the area was Coalition on Revival, a group of pastors and lay leaders who were from many different denominations. These people were meeting to pray for revival in Cincinnati. I was invited to be part of this—another commitment, but exciting to see black and white pastors together sharing their unique experiences and dreams.

My evenings were filled with planning. My husband was so gracious to give me his support and encouragement, because this was definitely taking time from him and the children since I was still working full time. By the end of 1993 into the beginning of 1994, all the commitments of family, work, and church were starting to overwhelm me. In March of 1994 I decided to retire early so I could spend more time with my family and more time on my church work. Was that ever a good decision! As the time grew closer to the conference weekend in August, I was amazed at how much time was needed to oversee all the details of a big conference. I had opportunities to speak before a few groups and to share the dream and encourage attendance at the conference. I might add that many pastors tried to discourage me from having this conference during the summer, stating hardly anyone would attend because summer was a bad time to get a large group of people together. Yet we persevered, trusting God would be in charge. We prayed and prayed. We even piled up all the invitations to many, many churches and organizations and prayed over them before mailing them.

Through contact with a person connected with a local radio station, I was asked to be interviewed one morning about the conference and specifically about Cindy Jacobs coming as the main speaker. I prepared my five minute talk and blithely went to the studio where I discovered I would be on for fifteen minutes. Fortunately, it was a question-and-answer type interview and most of the questions were given to me beforehand. I had never done this before—ever!

During the course of the briefing before going on the radio, the host expressed the belief that I had been the author of the book, and he thought he was getting a celebrity on the program. Now didn't that just help my old ego! Funny, but it just rolled over me and I explained my role in the whole situation. His comment was, "Well, we will simply fill the time talking about prayer." *What could be better?* I thought. As the live interview began, the Lord helped me through it. I did not stumble or hunt for words; they just seemed to flow easily. But then at the end the interviewer asked me, "What do you plan to do for a follow-up of this conference after all these people are brought together to be reconciled?"

That had not been a rehearsed question and I had never given that a thought. You can't take too long to answer on live radio, so I immediately asked in my thoughts, *Help me, Holy Spirit,* and out of my mouth came, "We will have an evening of praise and worship, inviting all those who attended the conference to come. We can share experiences of how God touched lives during that event." After I left the interview, I put those thoughts on hold and proceeded with the continuing mountain of details for the conference, again blithely unaware of how God was going to use that event down the road.

As the time drew near for the conference I became even more excited. All the women working with me had been so helpful. We received all kinds of help from volunteers at our churches. Everything was in place. The day before the event was to be held a group of intercessors prayed over the entire area and for all the speakers, musicians, and coordinators of the conference. This prayer covering was for the entire twenty-four hours before the event began. I picked up Cindy Jacobs at the airport. What a bubbling personality this woman has. Her face reflected peace, joy, and radiance that were almost tangible. During our conversation she informed me that it had been a while since she had spoken at churches to small groups (hundreds). The Lord had been calling her to large conferences with thousands of people interceding in the spiritual realm for reconciliation among races. However, in her many prayers seeking God's direction, it was made evident to her that she should come to Cincinnati. During the conference she shared that God had a particular plan for this city and we would be a light on the hill, a place of refuge. Of course, Cincinnati is known to be the city of seven hills. What a beautiful vision that God's love would shine out on the hills of our city with love and unity of denominations and races.

God was good and there were hundreds of people attending the conference, even from other cities. Naturally, this type of gathering resulted in many different churches being represented and many different worship styles. As the chairperson up front introducing musicians, pastors, and Cindy Jacobs at each session,

I often noticed the varying poses of people during the worship and praise times and also during the times of corporate prayer. I made the remark that people should feel free to lift their hands or to sit quietly—however the Holy Spirit led them. I must have mentioned that, even though I did not raise my hands, it was joyful to see the spontaneity of those who did.

After the conference I received a letter from a pastor of a Pentecostal church thanking me for the wonderful time with the Lord. In that letter he told me there would come a time when the Lord would give me the freedom to worship in the style of hand raising. And it did come to pass—a prophetic word—uplifting—and accepted. In fact, by the year 2000, I not only loved to raise my hands in praise but also enjoyed using flags as a way of praise and feeling free to clap my hands when singing specific songs. This came from the woman who used to grab the pew in front of her with white-knuckled hands to keep from being noticed.

During the conference, Cindy Jacobs' main thrust of speaking was on reconciliation. I had not realized the depth of bigotry or racial division until I heard her talks over the two-day period. Many people came to the front of the sanctuary seeking forgiveness and giving forgiveness for past hurts. It was a beautiful and moving time. On Saturday afternoon, Cindy Jacobs ended her talk and invited people to come forward for individual prayer. Remember, there were hundreds of people there. She asked for some men to stay with her and act as "catchers." That was a new term for me. Just in case it is new for you also, this means to be available, standing behind the person being prayed for, to catch the person if they should fall under the power of the Spirit. The catcher gently lowers the person to the floor. What does it mean, falling under the power of the Spirit? To the best of my understanding as a person is praying for you, the power of the Holy Spirit simply flows through the person praying into the person receiving. The power is so overwhelming that the person simply cannot stand up under the onslaught. It is sometimes referred to as "being slain in the Spirit."

I watched many people going forward. I saw many, many people falling to the ground. And I thought, *Well, this won't happen to me, because I don't particularly believe in that.* But at the same time I thought I should go up for prayer because I was the chairperson and it might offend Cindy Jacobs if I didn't. So up I went. She came over to me. She did not touch me. She simply said, "Evelyn, be filled with the joy of the Lord. Fill her, Lord, with Your joy."

Down I went. To this day I can remember the sensation of heaviness of limbs. There was no way I could lift my arms or my head or my body. As I was lying there on the floor I sensed I was smiling. The smile seemed to be radiating throughout my whole body. A sensation washed over my entire being that was totally unexplainable. Finally, as I started to rise up, Cindy Jacobs glanced over at me. She smiled and said, "More, Lord. More joy." And she pointed her hand at me. I simply fell right back down flat on the floor. I have no idea how long I was there. But I can assure you reader, there was no pushing, no magic, no pulling from behind by the catchers. No person had touched me—but God had.

From that day on I have had a sense of joy in my spirit that continues to bring me through times of difficulty, days of sadness, times of things not going my way particularly. I know the joy in my spirit must come through in my teaching because often those attending a class will mention the joy they see in me. I want so badly to share this joy with others. I want others to receive this joy so they can enjoy every single day on this earth that the Lord gives us. The joy of the Lord creates a sparkle in our eyes, a smile on our lips, and a spring in our steps. The blessing of joy is given when we find Jesus and know Him, not just as the Son of God and our Savior, but also as our personal friend, our intercessor with God. He then becomes the role model for how to live our lives on this earth. And Scripture promises us when we follow Jesus and believe in him we have abundant life, a life of joy. (1 Pet. 1:8.)

This was the biggie for me at the conference. At least that was what I thought at the moment. Remember, I started out planning this whole conference because I thought it would be a nice thing to do. Yet the Lord was beginning to show me that His marvelous plan was only just beginning to unfold.

Reconciliation and Ministry Calling

I asked Cindy Jacobs if she would autograph my copy of her book, *Possessing the Gates of the Enemy.* She graciously did, and the words she wrote were "To Evelyn—God's anointed prayer warrior—called to reconciliation."

I agreed with her calling me a prayer warrior. I had heard that said of me on more than one occasion. But called to reconciliation? What would that entail? Where would I start? Was God calling me to that kind of ministry?

Remember when I was being interviewed by the radio station and had to give a follow-up idea? Before the conference, since I had committed over the airwaves to a special service, our committee talked about how we could do this. We made up flyers to pass out at the conference inviting all who attended to come to the praise service. It would be held at my church. We planned to have Pastor Mike lead the service and also have a nondenominational pastor lead all the worship music. Since this was to be a reconciliation praise service, I thought there should be pastors of different races involved in leading the service. I did not know any black pastors on a personal basis. I did remember that one of the pastors in the COR (Coalition on Revival) group

I mentioned earlier was a worship leader. Pastor Mike knew him and suggested he might be willing to be involved in this service. I got the phone number, called, and left a message stating who I was and what I wanted to talk about. Pastor Shawn McMullen called me back, and after talking for a while, said he would be willing to lead in the worship time.

Our plan was to have a lengthy time of praise music where we would all join together in song and Pastor McMullen would share thoughts to draw us into a deeper worship in whatever way the Holy Spirit led him. Pastor Mike would lead in prayer. We would have a time where people could come to the microphone and share how they were touched by the conference. There would be a time to fellowship with one another. The evening came. There were so many churches represented with more than one hundred people attending. By the time the service concluded, there was great fellowship between all those attending. In fact, people did not leave until almost 10:00 P.M., and the service had started around 7:00 P.M. Pastor McMullen shared with me that he thought we should have more of these kinds of services. With Pastor Mike, Pastor McMullen, Dotty Mack, and me meeting several times to plan how this service should flow, we eventually held three more of these praise and fellowship services. It was continually a joy to see so many black and white brothers and sisters in Christ Jesus worshipping together, talking to one another, hugging and laughing and just generally being comfortable with one another. These services opened my eyes to how differently people worship and yet how much alike we truly are as brothers and sisters in Christ Jesus. How can we be reconciled to God if we are not reconciled to our brothers and sisters of a different race? How can we serve the Lord in honesty and humility if we hold deep within our hearts grudges or dislike for another race? I didn't have answers at that time, but I sure had the questions.

I will never forget one man who testified to what God had done in removing hatred from his heart during the conference who came up to me and said, "Sister, have you realized that we cannot say the name "Jesus" softly? No matter how we try, it comes out strong and powerful. Don't you imagine how terrified the demons are when they see us worshipping Jesus together?" His name was Adam. And, yes, I agree with him. In fact, I have shared that comment in my teaching more than once. What a beautiful thought.

As a result of these services, I thought more and more about a ministry of reconciliation. I contacted a member of our church, Dotty Mack. Dotty is a good friend. She is also a black woman, and I believed she would be a great asset to starting a ministry on reconciliation and revival for our city. She agreed to work with me on this. We decided to call this ministry, "R & R for God's People." R & R stood for Revival and Reconciliation. We formed a prayer group meeting twice a month to pray for our city in these areas. The members included both black and white races and several denominations. Eventually, through the suggestion of Pastor Mike, we started holding prayer times twice a month in nursing homes. This particular area of ministry seemed to be a calling for Dotty and now, ten years later, she holds these prayer meetings at four different nursing homes twice a month. They are open to all interested people of any race. This ministry has never grown into some big well-known or well-publicized ministry. Dotty and I faithfully serve in this ministry as God continues to call us. It has been ten years since the beginning of this bonding of friendship between Dotty and me. To this day we both continue praying for our city, pastors, the church, reconciliation, and God to bring revival.

We study God's Word together. We play golf together during the summer time. We are prayer partners—meaning we pray for each other every single day, year after year. I have anguished over how to tell you about this part of my growing in Christ Jesus and how I have been called to something so completely out of my previous experience. I have no grandiose answers to the big problem of racial unrest. I do not want to get into the political correctness of the problem. So how do I share what has happened in my life as God touched my heart during that conference?

I was visiting my daughter Camille in New Jersey, and one day I told her that each time I tried to write this chapter it sounded stilted and dull. She asked, "Well, how do you really feel about this ministry God has called you to?" I started telling her what I felt, and Camille said, "You should hear the passion in your voice, Mom, as you explain how you feel. Why not write what you just shared with me?"

The following are some of the thoughts I expressed to Camille. I will try to explain how the last six years of my life have changed in opening my eyes and heart to the black community. I have found friendships that are so delightful—such a blessing to me. I have learned that when a black person calls me Sister, that is a sign of respect for an older woman. When a black friend calls me Sis, that indicates her acceptance of me. I have been in meetings where black people have opened their hearts to the kinds of hurt they experience. For instance, one young woman shared when she is in an elevator she feels as though she is invisible. One time, just recently, I was at a customer service desk in a department store. The older black woman who was waiting on me had to take a call. She looked at me while talking and after hanging up said, "That person wanted to speak to the colored boy in one of the departments." What do you say to a black person that has just been put down by an unthinking remark? I have visited black churches and enjoyed their enthusiastic worship style. In most white churches people have a tendency to dress casually. Not in the black churches I have visited. I mentioned to one of my friends how I noticed they all dressed so formally. Her comment, "Sis, we are coming before the king. Would you not dress in your best if you were going to be in the presence of a king?" I have grown to understand that the color of our skin doesn't make us any different when it comes to honesty, family relationships, friendship, and dreams. However I also have come to realize that being white is very different from being a person of color. I never thought about the color of my skin. If I wasn't accepted at a particular club or organization, so what? I could care less. I always felt equal to anyone. I never realized there were people who didn't experience this confidence in who they were and their lack of acceptance in society as an equal.

In my exchange of ideas with white people regarding the black community as a whole, often there is definitely a lack of understanding or inability to relate to what the black people have experienced over many generations, and this saddens me. I only know that for me, the friendships I have formed over these past few years are highly treasured. I would trust my life to these dear women. Their love for the Lord is deep and honest. How I love to worship the Lord with them! So, when I hear unfair remarks, I just have to share my thoughts about the subject. It breaks my heart when I hear unkind remarks made about a race as a whole. Do people sometimes look at me funny? Yes. Does it make me feel bad? No. If I do not stand up for what I believe, how can I serve in the manner the Lord has laid on my heart? I try very hard to make it a personal observation and encourage thinking of the situation as a one-on-one issue. This often seems to allow the person to rethink what they have said as an all encompassing race issue. I pray for our city to become accepting of all peoples. Of course, there are those who do bad things. This is true of any race. But surely God's Word is true, and my understanding is that God loves all people. We are equal in His sight, not one race better than another. But for many people who do not have a love for the Lord, this is not a truth they accept. I don't know how this can be resolved except through constant prayer that God will move in the hearts of people.

I think God has used this call on my life to show me how to love people for who they are, regardless of the color of their skin or the denomination of their church, and, yes, even for the unbeliever. It has given me great joy and freedom to worship with the lifting of my hands in praise or clapping to a joyful praise song, to using flags in worship, and to letting my feet dance to the beautiful music during our prayer meetings or at some conferences or when I visit my friends' churches.

I want to share here how the Lord often orchestrates the plan He has for us when we are willing to try to fulfill it. When I felt led to start this ministry and Dotty came on board with me, we chose the name through much prayer and discussion. This was after the praise and worship services resulting from the conference. As I mentioned before, Dotty and I met with Pastor McMullen and Pastor Mike several times to discuss the two sides of the issue. What insights I gathered. Then it was time to decide how to carry out this new ministry. From my exposure to a good many pastors citywide, I decided to contact a black pastor from a church in another part of the city. I called him and asked if we could meet at my church. On the appointed day, I shared with him what I believed the Lord was calling me to do. I explained I had no idea how to make this happen. I told him what I felt and how I believed prayer to be the focal point of the ministry. The pastor, Rev. Gallen Jones, said apparently I had been listening to the Spirit, and he agreed with what Dotty and I were trying to put into place. He told me he could not be part of it, but knew of an intercessor at his church who also had a heart for reconciliation and revival. He would call her and explain and get back to me.

When Rev. Jones called me the next week he gave me the name of a lady, Lucille. This lady was interested in talking to me. I called her, we talked, and she said she would love to come to the prayer time but because of eye problems could not drive. Now, here is the part where God has to do a work in us for reconciliation. There was a questioning, a trust level, and a sincerity that needed to be worked out in both of us. I didn't know this lady or anything about her, but I offered to pick her up as she did not live too far away. She was allowing a woman she didn't know to drive her to a place she had never been before. This was nine years ago. We have become sisters in Christ Jesus. She has much godly wisdom and we have such fun together. I have come to respect the wisdom the Lord has given her, to be inspired by her enthusiasm and holy boldness. So often we express a thought and the other has been thinking the same thing. A Presbyterian and a Pentecostal—a white woman and a black woman, but we do have all things in common. We are both mothers and grandmothers. We care about others. We both have hearts for prayer and a deep love for Jesus. If I had not been invited to be part of the pastor's group, not met Pastor Jones, not called him and met with him to ask advice, would any of this have happened? How wonderful our God is to lead us into what He desires for us, if we but listen. There is a faithful group of six women representing four churches and two races that have been meeting together twice a month for many years to pray that our city becomes a place of reconciliation and for hearts to be open for God to bring revival.

One of the most rewarding things about our dedication to meeting and praying twice a month, is the compassion of our God to minister to each of us by the wonderful infilling of the Holy Spirit. Each of the six of us has been called to specific areas of ministry during our years of praying together. These ministries include visiting and praying with inmates of the Juvenile Justice Center; visiting and praying with people in nursing homes; teaching and counseling; being involved in support of encouraging Jewish people to open their hearts to Jesus the Messiah; speaking about prayer before groups, teaching, writing. Each one has been called to the ministry of intercession and reconciliation. Each has a deep longing for God to bring revival in her church, not just in our city but over our whole nation. Lucille and I are also prayer partners.

In the year 2002, Pastor Mike asked me if I would like to attend a meeting downtown regarding a reconciliation theme. We went together and listened to a man named Ford Taylor express his desire to form a House of Prayer in Cincinnati and to begin a deeper relationship between races and denominations. The ministry was being called "Transformation Cincinnati." He had moved here from Texas at the direction of the Lord because he felt this was what the Lord was calling him to do.

Transformation Cincinnati has established a "House of Prayer" downtown. They hold worship and prayer times and special events. There are many people involved in this ministry, including two of the women from our prayer group. I have not felt led to be a part of this and at first I wondered why. But I have come to the conclusion that God put a call on me to help pray it into being. Our group prayed faithfully for years for reconciliation and for God to bring out of the larger community a man to head this endeavor. One morning we prayed that God would send someone here from any part of the country to be the one to draw people together, and that is how we prayed from that time on. As I thought about what was happening with Transformation Cincinnati, I realized God had answered our prayers—and no doubt the prayers of many other groups over the years. Therefore, we no longer needed to meet together. I called the group together to share this and each one said they had been feeling the same way the past couple of months. We still see each other at special events, but we no longer meet. I have heard it said that sometimes God plans things for a season. What an awesome God we have. And His plan took eight years to become a reality. I feel humbled to have been a small part of it.

Another wonderful experience was opened up to me through being involved in a Bible Reading Marathon. This was held in our city for a number of years. In 1993, a black lady, Jerry

Mundy, who I had met several years before through one of the community prayer groups I attended, asked if our church would like to be involved. Of course, I agreed and proceeded to encourage people from our church to participate. Each person was assigned a specific time and specific scriptures to read for fifteen minutes. The marathon started on a Sunday afternoon and stopped on Thursday, the National Day of Prayer. It was held in front of the Courthouse in downtown Cincinnati. There is something so powerful about hearing the Word of God spoken over a microphone continuously.

That first day made a lasting impression upon me. For most of my life I have heard Scripture read aloud, but always in small segments. Never had I heard it read aloud continuously for four hours. What power is released! One could sense the Lord's presence. There was an absolute peace about the area. I sensed angels surrounding us, guarding us so there would be no heckling or unpleasantness. And there wasn't for the entire four hours I was there. As each person who came to read walked into the area, they brought with them a smile, a radiance, and an acceptance that we were all sisters and brothers in Christ Jesus. There were white people, black people, and Asian people. There were people from Evangelical churches, Pentecostal churches, and nondenominational churches.

We gathered in groups and prayed. We prayed for God's Word to touch people as they went by and for The Word to flow out into the street and dispel any evil spirits. We prayed for each person who was reading to be blessed as they read the Word aloud. We gave praise to Jesus and asked that God would be glorified. As we prayed, I realized we were truly praying in one spirit, just as Jesus desired when He expressed to God that we would be one in Him as He was one in God (John 17). It did not make any difference what church or denomination the person was from. In fact, that subject did not even come up. It was wonderful. There was evident caring and joining of hands and spirits in the groups of different races and denominations. At one point, Jerry Mundy's husband, Walter, started singing an old spiritual hymn as we stood in a circle of joined hands. It was beautiful and brought tears to my eyes. As the sun shined down on my face, I felt so warm and realized the sun is like the heat of the Holy Spirit. It reaches deep down inside and spreads warmth all the way to the fingertips and pours out caring, sharing, and love.

As God's Word was proclaimed, I noticed peoples' voices were so clear, so strong. I noticed that each person, after reading, appeared to be very moved by what he or she had done. Our circles of prayer must have been releasing the power of the Holy Spirit to bless each reader.

A man came over to listen. He probably was coming directly from his job as he had his window-cleaning tools with him. He wanted to tithe what he had. He held a handful of change and kept saying, "I want to tithe," and he put the change on the podium. So little, but to God, no doubt, it was so much. What words were proclaimed that had touched this man? We will probably never know, but something did. Later, an Asian man came up to us and asked, "What is this all about? What church? A fundamentalist?" We told him no particular church, just people from many churches all together in unity reading the Word of God. "That is really nice. Just lots of churches?" he said. And he kept nodding as if to say "this is good." An interesting observation was that almost all the people who came to listen were men. Most of these men gave the appearance of not having a lot of personal income. However, there appeared to be a hunger for something more than they had as they listened in rapt attention. Little incidents, yet these one-on-one interchanges might just be the start of an understanding or reconciliation between two people. And better yet, perhaps this was the beginning of a deeper hunger and understanding of our compassionate, merciful God. Our church was involved with this Bible Reading Marathon for several years, and each time it was a wonderful experience.

I am sure that the Lord will continue to show me new understandings and new thoughts about reconciliation throughout my life. Perhaps I will even have the opportunity to make additional friendships with people from other races. It is very difficult to put into words how this part of my ministry has affected my whole ministry of prayer and teaching. It has certainly taught me much about humility versus ego. It has opened for me a new area of joy. It has created in my heart a deeper understanding of compassion for those in different life situations than mine. It has heightened my awareness of how the spoken word hurts. It has helped me respond to others with a smile, a recognition by eye contact, a simple thank you for a service rendered. Isn't it amazing how our God takes us into new areas of experiences and opens up new beginnings when we are willing to allow Him to mold us and change us? Each day becomes an opportunity to allow God to use me in some small way to reach out with love for one or more of His people. Even as I write this, my eyes well with tears of joy for how God has taken a very reserved, private-type woman, and placed her into situations where emotions and thoughts are openly expressed. I am continually amazed by how God uses my words to minister through the power of the Holy Spirit to touch another's life. It has been impressed upon my heart to always, always acknowledge that it is not just my doing, it is by the power of the Holy Spirit. I am simply a vessel through which the Holy Spirit touches a person or eases a situation. And you know what? It is freeing to realize I don't have to know all the answers. I don't have to resolve situations. I don't have to change people's lives. But I do have to be willing to be used as the Lord directs. The Holy Spirit has brought me to a point in my life where this is a welcome call. It is absolute joy to serve the Lord as He directs. I thought this might be a good time to share one of my poems about reaching out in boldness rather than putting off something that God might have planned especially for His children.

"Today Is the Day"

How often I plan something, thinking I will do it for
the Lord.
But things come up and I say, "Tomorrow, Lord, I will
do it tomorrow."
But the Lord says, "Today is the day!"

For each day is new. Each day an opportunity that comes
but once.
If we accept the challenge and step forth into the
unknown today,
What might it bring us? If we pull back, what might
we have missed?

The Lord holds out so much joy for us, so many
challenges.
Yet always there is the enemy lurking in the shadows
To discourage us, to tell us we are not able,
To pull us away from our God.
Do we listen to what is in the darkness?
Or do we listen to what is in the light?

For the light is Jesus, and that Light overcomes the
darkness.
Let us grasp the challenge and say to ourselves, today,
Lord.
This is the day planned for me to become closer to my
Lord.
This is the day God has planned something special for
me.
I don't want to miss it.

Help me, oh Holy Spirit, to have the courage to grab
the challenge
And run with it through the valleys, over the hills, always
remembering
That You are with me, Lord God, and love me with an
everlasting love.
That You will never reject me. That You created me to
be your child.
I wait for whatever challenge You put before me.
Lord God, is today the day?

Written October 29, 1996

To end this chapter I want to share a vision I had on May 6, 1995. I was praying about the reconciliation ministry and asking for clarity and guidance. I remember that my head was lifted and I was gazing out the family room window. I saw a vision of deadwood. All the wood was filled with holes and was consumed by fire and disappeared. Then I saw arms of all colors linked together in a huge circle, and I knew there were praises coming from this linkage of races. In the center of this circle where the deadwood had been were churches, and they had no roofs. From out of these churches came a marvelous radiance floating from the roofless tops, merging into a singleness. Reader, do you not think this must be the desire of God's heart, that we believers all be linked together in praise to Him who is able and mighty and just and forgiving and loving, forever and ever?

CHAPTER 12

Deeper Understanding of God's Calling

During 1995, I attended more conferences. Each one impacted my life in a new way. In January of that year I was asked to attend a conference in Kentucky for Assembly of God ministers and lay leaders. I thought this would be interesting and could possibly give me an opportunity to see how another denomination expresses their worship and leadership in a larger setting. Little did I know where the Holy Spirit was going to lead me. You would think by this time I would be expecting a bolt of lightning to hit me. Not me. I just think, *this might be interesting,* and away I go. However, I do always take notes and make observations, for I believe the Holy Spirit guides me into things that I would not otherwise see or remember. And of course, now I realize I needed the thoughts for this book.

The main speaker was a lady named Dr. Mary Stewart Relfe. She is a woman of prayer and has a heart for revival. She felt called to form a "League of Prayer" ministry that teaches people to pray for revival. It is based in Alabama. Dr. Relfe has written a book titled, *Cure of All Ills.* She speaks to many groups around the country. During the last day of the conference Dr. Relfe began speaking about dedicating a segment of time to prayer each day.

She called us to give one hour every day to the Lord in prayer and invited people to come forward and commit to this. I was standing at my seat, music was playing softly, and I was saying in my mind, *No way can I do this. I certainly cannot commit a whole hour every day to praying. What would I pray about for that long?* As I was arguing this with the Holy Spirit, my feet were literally moving out of the row and down the aisle, and I found myself standing in a large group of people. I couldn't believe I was standing there. "Can I really do this, Lord?" I asked. As you can imagine, I felt overwhelmed and scared, yet determined. I made the commitment.

I looked around at the huge number of people who had come forward. There were men leaning against the walls, kneeling, crying, their faces in their hands. There was that beautiful sound of harmony as people prayed in tongues. I was aware of how the Holy Spirit convicts us to give of ourselves, often in ways we never dreamed.

After I came home and prayed about this commitment, I made the promise that I would pray every Monday through Saturday for at least one hour. Sunday would be the time I spent with God at church. At first I was so organized. I made up a folder entitled Prayer Requests and kept the folder in a drawer close to my favorite praying spot. I did this because I still couldn't imagine I would find enough to pray about for one whole hour. However, it wasn't long before situations were given to me or I saw situations in a different light or the Holy Spirit laid a specific situation on my heart, and the prayer list was always plenty long enough to cover the commitment of sixty minutes. As I grew more comfortable spending so much time with the Lord in prayer, I realized I had taken the promise of spending one hour too literally. Now, I don't always pray the entire sixty minutes at one sitting. I have found that as the years have gone by, my prayers are almost continual. I can be driving my car and see a situation that speaks to my heart and pray.

As I mentioned earlier, for some reason every time I pass a group of men working in an open man hole, I feel called to pray for their safety. Why? I don't know, but I do it in obedience, believing the Holy Spirit has prompted the urge to pray for those men. The person doesn't know, but God does. I pray as I work around the house. Lots of my prayers are just giving God praise for His goodness. I belong to a weekly prayer group. Prayers are said during every committee meeting I attend. I belong to the reconciliation/revival prayer group. I have a number of prayer partners. These are people who are committed to praying for one another each day, all year long. People call me on the telephone asking for special prayers. I pray for concerns periodically on the church electronic prayer line. At times I pray for a situation shown on TV News. At times I have been engaged in a worldly activity and the urge to pray for a person or situation comes to mind. I pray silently at that very moment, trusting God knows why the prayer is needed.

As I write this I realize anew how God never calls us to a specific way of serving Him or a seeming sacrifice of our time, that He doesn't actually fulfill the requirements needed for serving. And best of all, God rewards us with a sense of contentment and peace about what He calls us to do. I feel very honored when a person calls me on the telephone and asks me to pray for a situation.

Early in 1995, I asked Dotty Mack if she would like to attend a conference with me in Leesburg, Virginia, from June 28 through July 3. This conference was held by Intercessors for America. Dotty and I prayed about it and decided to go for the last three days, anticipating a growth time in our prayer lives. From the very beginning I realized the enemy was putting up road blocks. We flew to Leesburg in a small commuter plane with only twelve people on the flight. Upon arrival at Dulles airport, Dotty's baggage was lost. After settling that problem, we blissfully went to the phones to call the hotel for a van to pick us up. The hotel was not listed. The information desk did not know about any such hotel. I called the 800 number given by the conference people and was given the name and phone number of the hotel along with the promise of a van to pick us up right away. After thirty minutes of waiting, the van arrived and took us to the hotel. It was in an office complex and did not look like hotels usually do. We went to the desk and the clerk said, "You were supposed to be here June 28, and that is why the van was not there to get you." Apparently wrong information had been given as we arrived on June 30. About this time their intercom came on with a voice saying, "Get someone to room —- with a plunger. The toilet is running over." About a minute later another call came over the intercom, saying; "This is room —-, we need help; the shower rod just fell down." The clerk looked at us and said, "Are you sure you want to check in here?" In my mind, I am thinking, *No, no!* There was not another soul to be seen in this hotel. Well, we finished checking in and went to our room, which was very nice. I called the conference people for a shuttle to where the conference was being held. Dead silence, then; "You want us to pick you up?"

"Yes," I said. "This was the understanding when we registered in May." We were picked up and taken to the conference center, and the rest of the day was fine. That evening, again the look of panic when we stopped at the desk to get the shuttle back to the hotel. A young woman was standing there. Dotty had been talking to her during the afternoon. She volunteered to take us to the hotel and pick us up the next morning. Wonderful! I asked the conference person if there was a room available where the conference was being held. She was able to accommodate us, and we transferred to the conference area the next morning. The rest of the conference was fine until we got ready to leave on Sunday. We had made a reservation with the shuttle group to leave the conference at 2:45 P.M. At 12:45 P.M. I heard an announcement that the only shuttles leaving for the airport were at 1:00 P.M. and 4:00 P.M. We had exactly fifteen minutes to dash to the next building, finish packing, check out, and get to the building where the shuttle was. Amazingly, we made it. When we arrived at 6:18 P.M. in Cincinnati, guess what? They had lost my luggage. I remember telling the clerk at the lost and found desk, "I don't care about my clothes, but you had better find my Bible." Satan did his best to deter us from enjoying or entering into the spirit of the conference, which was wonderful. But we just kept praising God and saying, "God will take care of it." I have never taken a trip anywhere, anytime, that I have encountered so much harassment. Of course, we both got our luggage back in good time.

I am going to share the thoughts I jotted down during the three-day conference. Little did I realize I would be sharing any of these with others years later.

Friday afternoon, June 30, 1995: The first workshop speaker we heard was John Anderson. He had written a new book called The Cry of Compassion, *and he and his wife head a ministry called Cry of the Innocents. Mr. Anderson had been in New Zealand and Australia for the past six years. After being out of our country for six years and returning, his heart was like a volcano, causing his heart to cry out to God in grief for this nation. As he talked about this, he actually had tears in his eyes and his voice quivered. One of the statements he made touched me. "We are defined by our sins and our sins define our country." I was listening to a man who was so grieved by how our nation seemed to be turning away from absolutes and the truth of the Lord. At the end of his talk, I prayed in silence, "Lord, spare us from war or whatever could result from our indifference." And I heard in my spirit, "Spare you for what?"*

He mentioned God is giving our nation a wake-up call. I heard this repeatedly throughout the weekend.

The next workshop speaker was Alan Keyes, one of the Republican presidential candidates. What a heart for God this man has! He spoke much about the Declaration of Independence and how this country must get back to focusing on what the declaration states and to carrying it out. His talk was very inspiring. At the end of the workshop, I turned to Dotty and said, "I don't believe God will place Mr. Keyes in the presidential seat. I think it would be too hard to carry out the passion for God he has in that political environment. Yet I believe God has a very special work for Mr. Keyes to fulfill."

The last speaker of that day was Johannes Facius from the Holland/Germany area of Europe. He is a former pastor and author of God Can Do It Without Me, *which explains about intercession. He was very low-key and taught much about the Lord's commission to us and how he sees the importance of America's need to return to putting God first in everything.*

Saturday, July 1: I was excited to have the opportunity to hear Bill Bright speak. He is founder and president of Campus Crusade for Christ International. He has written a wonderful book, The Coming Revival, *which explains America's call to fast, pray, and seek God's face. At this conference, Bill Bright is seventy-four years old. He was full of enthusiasm, had a young-looking appearance, and a strong voice. He shared he believes God is all. He gave the appearance of being very humble, giving God the credit for how he is being used to bring people to Jesus Christ.*

We had choices of workshops to attend. I chose to hear Grace Madigan, founder and director of Scepter of His Favor Ministries. This was a prayer workshop for women. Ms. Madigan did a lot of powerful praying according to the needs put on the hearts of the women present. One of the statements she made which impressed me was, "If you love the Lord, you will know how to love your husband. If you love the Lord, you will know how to love your children." This seemed to me to be a very thought-provoking statement. Later during the conference I had an opportunity to talk to her for a brief time. She asked if she could pray for me. Of course, I said yes. She prayed for the Lord to fill me with a holy boldness. What a lovely blessing prayer to ask for me.

The final speaker that so impressed me was Rev. Lloyd Ogilvie, Chaplain of the U. S. Senate and former pastor of First Presbyterian Church in Hollywood, California. What excitement he brought to his talk with us. What a charisma he has. His love for the Lord was so evident in his spoken word. What intellect and understanding and compassion he has for God's people. I was literally hanging on every word. He is an author that has influenced my walk with the Lord greatly over the years. I have taught an adult book study on his wonderful book, The Greatest Counselor In the World, *which teaches on the Holy Spirit. I highly recommend it.*

Throughout the conference there were times of very special worship with anointed worship leaders. On Sunday morning, after an extended worship and praise time, the issue of racial reconciliation was brought forth. After some corporate praying, one of the speakers expressed a sense that there should be corporate repentance and forgiveness to bring about intercessory reconciliation. The speaker asked all the black attendees to come up on the platform to stand in the gap for their race. My friend Dotty said she felt she had been doing this enough in our own city and was going to stay with me. I suggested that, on the contrary, this might be the very reason God encouraged her to attend the conference, and I thought she should go up front. She did. What a time of repentance. Pastors from other countries were asking forgiveness of slave trade. There was much weeping and people falling to their knees in prayer. I noticed that of all the people standing up there representing the black race, Dotty had such a glow about her and the stream of people waiting to speak to her was very long. After a time of praying for God to intervene in this nation-wide problem, I felt led to walk forward and stand by Dotty. We held hands and sang and prayed together. What a tremendous feeling of sisterly love and bonding was happening between us. What a blessed way to end the conference.

I want to mention here that at times you might attend a conference, seminar, or a one-day or one-evening event and feel as if you didn't get much out of it. Or perhaps you didn't agree with what was said. Or maybe you felt uncomfortable with the worship style, etc. This has happened to me more than once. At times I have even wanted to get up and leave. I could not enter into the spirit of the worship time. Or I kept thinking that this person's thoughts seem to be moving away from the scripture as I have been taught to interpret. After one such evening, the next morning I was still feeling unease. In fact, I could not seem to settle down and do anything else but just continually rehash what I had experienced. I called Lucille, the friend I mentioned earlier in this book who I believed to be very wise in this area and explained how I was feeling. She told me this was not unusual when one has been given the gift of discernment. She said I should ask the Lord to take away any thoughts He did not want me to remember and enjoy the good things I learned or experienced. She also said I should expect to not always agree with all I would hear over the years from guest speakers. I considered this wise counsel and have decided that any time I feel really uncomfortable I will leave during a break. Otherwise, I will sort out and hang on to the good information I receive.

I mention this in case you might at some point run into the same type situation and think there was something wrong with you. You are probably just receiving the gift of discernment and need to think more about that particular subject. The Lord could even be encouraging you to study that particular issue more in-depth for a reason not understood at the time. I have come to realize God uses people in different ways to reach different cultures or lifestyles or intellects. I should not question or worry so much about methods but should always question that the truth of God's Holy Word, the sovereignty of our God, the Lordship of Jesus Christ, and the indwelling of the Holy Spirit is preached.

Over the years I attend fewer and fewer big conferences. I prefer an all-day or an evening speaker. It was certainly important for me in the beginning to attend the large conferences as I was learning much about various ways of worship, hearing from men and women God had touched for a very special ministry, and it also helped me be more open to receiving whatever God wanted to reveal to me for my own serving Him later on. Often when we attend any such event, whether it is a few hours or a whole weekend, we have been nudged to attend so the Holy Spirit can give us a special anointing or a fresh, deeper anointing in serving. I usually come away from the event feeling uplifted and joyful that I have been in the presence of so many people of God.

CHAPTER 13

Insights on God's Love for Me

One morning during the summer of 1995, I had been pray-ing and basking in God's presence. Suddenly thoughts started rushing through my mind. I quickly jotted them down. Some of these thoughts were: God truly danced the day I was born, just as He does for each of His children. He rejoices when I call on Him and ask for His guidance or when I pray deep in my spirit to hear Him, to just bask in who He is. He rejoices when I take time to think about the magnificence of what He has done and will do for all those who believe in Him and His promise to be wherever I am at all times. He guards me with angels and His Holy Spirit because He is a God who loves His children—equally—regardless of color, creed, age, culture, or intellect. Jesus not only sacrificed His life for our salvation but also that we might enjoy Him today, tomorrow, and forever.

You might be thinking, *Well, I already know that and from what the writer has been sharing, she should know that.* What was being shown to me and what I want to share with you is that I had reached a point where it was all coming together. I had begun to know and accept that everything I had experienced, all that I had been taught, was real. It was true. I was actually beginning to understand what it means to walk with Jesus. I had begun to realize that I am loved without reservation.

As the summer passed, I found myself enjoying the hour dedicated each day to focusing on the Lord. I found the Holy Spirit bringing to my conscious mind things I had done or not done many years previously. I sought forgiveness, and from that a breaking down of more barriers of aloofness began. My daily thoughts and actions often centered more on others than just on self. Of course, I could do this more easily because all the children were grown and away from home. I believed my relationship with the Lord was deepening, and I was just beginning—and I do mean beginning—to understand the depth of His love for all His children. I realized that the more I surrendered self, my pride, my feeling that I knew best, and sought the advice and guidance of the Holy Spirit, the more I allowed the Lord to use me. I was able to understand scriptures with excitement and a desire to share the wonder of God's Holy Word. I was allowing the Holy Spirit to be in tune with my heart and mind and soul. Such joy! Such exhilaration! Such expectancy!

These kinds of feelings seemed to just flow through me day after day. I have found that when I praise my God, it allows me to surrender self and that His thoughts pour into me without hindrance. Often I weep in my prayer time as I am led to pray for a people, a situation, or a nation. It is not crying as when we are sad or hurting or angry. It is more that my eyes tear and my heart feels so full of sadness that I must walk the floor or lie flat on the floor or kneel on the floor and pray until the feeling is released. Sometimes I feel called to pray for the lost and sense the utter hopelessness of many or the fears, the violence, the wanton destruction, the disregard for life, the missed chance to live for all the aborted babies, the shedding of innocent blood, the degradation of women, the waste of life itself, the turning away from God's absolutes. I sense the enemy is pulling out all the stops and only God can solve these heavy problems.

So I pray, and pray again. Do I feel it is hopeless? No. For I believe God calls us to pray. He desires our prayers. Often He does not act until prayer is lifted up. Prayer is a strong weapon against the enemy who tries to cause us to give up by creating conflict, apathy, or discouragement. But we know our God is faithful. If we persevere in prayer, He will hear and answer. What a wonderful promise. And this comes from a woman who was questioning whether there was a God sixteen years earlier.

Throughout all the conferences I have attended, the different denominational church worship styles I have experienced, the study of God's Word, and the many Christian books and music I have been exposed to, one thing has continually come into focus for me. We need to praise God, Jesus, and the Holy Spirit more and more. Each time we give praise we are acknowledging the majesty of the triune God. I believe God truly inhabits the praises of His people, just as the Psalms tell us. The power of the Holy Spirit is released into us and through us as we praise God. This release of power can heal and cleanse and protect us. Praising our God is one of the secrets of releasing His power. We need to raise our expectations of what the Lord can do in the power of His Spirit. As we praise God and focus on who He is, the worthiness of the Lamb of God, the power of the Holy Spirit, we are taken into a deeper worship. At that point we become more open to receiving the blessings of God because true worship is one of the most healing places a believer can be. It allows us to be more sincere, to rejoice, to receive more truths and a deeper understanding of His power by lifting the veil from our eyes. It dispels fear and pours peace into our souls. How do I know this is true? The Book of Revelation, chapter 4, tells us that even the angels continually sing praises to Him who sits on the throne. There surely must be a song constantly flowing through heaven. And if God enjoys the praises in the place of perfection, how much more must He desire it here on earth from us! When we are praising our God, we are also dispelling the darkness around us. The light of Jesus shoves out the darkness and the praise resounds in glorifying the Lord.

Another thing that has been shown to me is the wonderful opportunity to receive a sense of peace and contentment even in the midst of strife. When I set aside time and focus or center on Jesus and allow the Holy Spirit to direct my thoughts, I find myself praising God and actually forming a deeper belief in His awesome majesty. In doing this, I am surrendering myself to the Lord. I am giving my time, my energy, and my thoughts—all that I am—to worshipping God. Do I get tired of doing this? Never! Do I do this every single day? No. But I do talk to Him, thank Him for protection, whatever is on my mind that day. Each evening before dinner I ask God's blessing on the food I am about to eat, and I thank Him for specific things that have happened during the day. Doing this brings to my conscious mind how often God touches situations that I would otherwise take for granted. I love doing this. It increases my joy in trusting God.

There really isn't a magic wand in life to make things go smoothly. There is a choice of following in the light of Jesus Christ or walking in the darkness of evil that really controls this world at present. Each of us makes this choice every single day—in fact, many times throughout each day. God created each of us to glorify Him, to walk with Jesus, to turn to God in all things, to allow the Holy Spirit to be our Counselor, and to be guided by the truth He speaks. When we refuse to do this we miss out on the joy and sense of love and contentment the Lord wants to give us. I have come to a point of belief in God's power, in the continual awareness of the Holy Spirit dwelling within me and His willingness to teach me, and above all to believe that Jesus died for my sins because He loved me so. We are given the ability to believe these things—if we so choose—and when we do, these beliefs help us through the troubles or fires of earth. The fires of earth can eventually be extinguished, but the all-consuming fire of God can never be extinguished. For the flame of light that is Jesus will always overpower the darkness of this world.

When this understanding became reality for me, it was a huge load lifted from my shoulders. I now face each day with eagerness. I know God is with me, watching over me, anticipating my willingness to choose to be with Him, to serve Him, and to love Him with all my heart, soul, mind, and strength. Is this easy? No. There are many, many days I struggle to give God His time. I procrastinate. I try to complete mundane chores. Yet, since I have given the Holy Spirit permission to give me a heightened awareness of God's calling, there is that feeling of unrest, an acknowledgment deep inside that I am breaking my promise. The time when I most feel God's presence is when I am totally focused in a prayerful attitude. Just sitting, listening, being. God blesses me with thoughts from the Holy Spirit. How do I know this? Because the words I hear in my mind are so different than I would speak, so much wiser than I usually think. I feel a comfort, a tremendous sense of love all around me. There is absolutely nothing I have ever experienced that compares. It is not at all like the love experienced between husband and wife. It is a love on a much higher plane, complete, and a profound revelation of what resulted in my life from the shed blood of Jesus. Remember, dear reader, Jesus shed His blood not just for me—but for each person reading this and for all those who haven't. Awesome, isn't it, that even before we were born into this world Jesus shed his blood for the sins we would commit? As I began to understand this, even just a little, the deep inner joy seemed to grow and grow. To this day it continues to grow. I continue to learn new things about our Lord. I still receive revelations as I study the Word. It is ever-new, ever-thrilling, ever-challenging, ever-exciting. I pray I will continue to learn until the day I die to this world.

Reader, I wrote an episode yesterday for this book. I skimmed over certain parts of what had happened and just shared the highlights. Last evening I felt convicted that I had been remiss in telling you all that happened. This morning is Sunday; the weather is so icy and cold and snowy that the church cancelled services. I can't remember this happening before. So I decided to spend some time in worship. I put on a praise tape and spent a joyful forty-five minutes giving praise to our Lord. As I was getting dressed, it came to me that I was choosing not to give you a complete account of what happened in the episode I had written about the day before. I was covering up my prideful ways. So here is the revised version. And by the way, I have prayed several times for guidance that all I put into this book will be true and factual to the best of my knowledge. This book is not being written to make me look good, but to share how God has touched my life and blessed me over and over.

On January 14, 1996, I was attending an evening of worship and praise at a nondenominational church here in Cincinnati. The speaker was Cindy Jacobs, who had come back to Cincinnati to speak at that church. Remember, she was the featured speaker for the conference that was the beginning of a big change in my life. Toward the end of the evening, there was such a feeling of the anointed presence of the Holy Spirit. Cindy Jacobs had been ministering to the body of believers for quite some time. I asked Lucille Simmons, my friend, if she wanted to go forward with me. When we finally got to the front line, I looked up at Cindy and could see the vitality had been drained from her face. The color and sparkle were gone. At that very moment she announced with a tearful voice she could not continue. Much as she wanted to, physically, she was finished. She assured us that the anointing was flowing through her to others and the ministry teams would continue to pray for people.

As I stood there, I thought that I really did not have a specific prayer request. I had come up because Cindy Jacobs was ministering. Perhaps I should just go back to my seat. Immediately the thought came that to do so would be rude to the ministry teams. I was giving the power to a person not to the Holy Spirit. It was not Cindy Jacobs in charge but the Holy Spirit. I was allowing pride to override the possibility of the Holy Spirit ministering to me. Thank goodness I realized a battle was being waged in my subconscious, and I stayed. A man came up to me and prayed in heavenly language, waved his hand back and forth to the side of me. Nothing happened. He moved on to Lucille, did basically the same thing, down she went under the power of the spirit. He stopped, looked at me and then came back to me again. He said something—I have no idea what it was—but he did not touch me. Down I went. This was only the second time this had happened to me. It was such a sweet time as I lie there on the floor. I could hear words immediately pouring into my mind and my heart. That was when I received the words at the very beginning of this book. I had been prayed for and was listening deeply for God's direction for me. I received it—again. "Write. You must start right away. Do not tarry. Do not be afraid. The words will flow like the water of a swift current that sparkles and glistens in the sun with a gentle roar. This is my word I say to you." As I got up, a great sense of peace washed over me. Such a sense of love covered me. I couldn't wait to get back to my seat and write down all the precious words I had received.

So how could I not obey? It is not easy to write about things that are held deep in one's heart. I realize there will be people who read this and scorn my hearing directions from the Lord in my heart—which is the intellect of my soul. You need to know that I continually struggle with the spirit of false pride. The enemy will constantly try to wiggle his negative thoughts into our minds. Pride is a very easy way for the enemy to increase our doubts or cause us to resist what the Lord wants for us. What if I had gone back to my seat? Would I have received the guidance I needed? Perhaps; but then again, perhaps not. I would never have known the delight of that moment if I had allowed my pride to take over. How right, how true things become, when the Holy Spirit is in charge. We are only the vessels He uses. If we are obedient, the Holy Spirit can use any of us. I have fought putting all this down on paper for more than seven years. I write a little, revise it, and then put it away for a month or so. Drag it out, write a little more, repeating the same pattern. Yet God has been faithful. When I do settle down and start writing, the words flow smoothly. I continue to be amazed at all the information right there in the journals into which I poured out my thoughts over many years. As I read over these entries, memories flood back, and with the understanding that the Holy Spirit has been giving me, I can share much in the way God has been growing me.

As I began to listen more and more to the direction of the Holy Spirit, I also realized I was being asked to do more and more in activities of the church. In the late 90s, some of the activities were not satisfying, even as I carried them out. A few areas that I had been asked to serve actually made me apprehensive. Finally, I went to the Lord in prayer. See, I continue to fall into the pattern of trying to make decisions on my own. I am, however, beginning to have a sense of unrest about some decisions and recognize I need God's direction. I was surprised at the responses I received as I listened for God's direction. "Do not take on anything new at this point. Remove yourself from areas of being in the limelight. You are to focus on teaching, prayer, and writing." I obeyed.

I started saying no to duties that I did not feel called to perform. And what a joy it has been to do those things God has planned for me. When teaching, how I love to share what is revealed to me in God's Word! I worried about my lack of a college degree as I would possibly teach those who have degrees. The Lord assured me with the words, "Trust in me with all your heart, and I will not let you down. I will give you strength. I will give you wisdom. I will give you inspiration. I will give you a refreshing. I will give you the joy."

And, dear reader, that promise has been with me and fulfilled in me every time I teach, every time I make a presentation, every time I meet with leaders regarding a special project. God is so faithful. And if I had to pick one thing that I have learned that helps me daily it is "to savor the moment." I have learned to enjoy little things that happen that perhaps others would think were of no consequence. But to me that particular happening is a joy, a delight, and an affirmation from the Lord of His great love for me.

Understand reader, we choose to either believe God can and does intervene and has a master plan for our lives or that everything falls by chance or coincidence or luck. I choose to believe God is in control. So many things happen that show me over and over God's love for me. One day, not too long after the glorious event I just shared with you, I felt really low, having a pity-me party. The day before had been a depressing day, and this day wasn't much better. At this point I thought, *The enemy is trying to spoil the joy I recently received.* So I rebuked the enemy in the name of Jesus. I thanked the Lord for His blessings. I asked the Lord to fill me anew with His Spirit. The telephone rang within minutes of this prayer. After I answered, this sweet voice said, "Jesus loves you." It was a church friend. When I told her I was not having a good day, she explained she had been nudged to call me and then asked if she could pray with me. Of course, I said yes. Coincidence? I don't think so. See how God uses us when we are obedient? This lady could have ignored the nudging. She was taking a chance that I would reject her encouragement. Yet her obedience in sharing those three words brightened my day.

These kinds of moments happen frequently. I accept and savor those moments, knowing our Lord is compassionate and merciful and loving—not just to me, dear reader—but to all His children who seek Him, call out to Him, and believe in Him.

I awoke one morning around the end of March in 1996 with a remnant of a dream hovering in my mind. It seemed I had been talking to the Lord and the words "I call who I call" kept flowing through my mind. I ate breakfast, made my bed, showered, dressed, and still the words tumbled around. Finally, I just sat on the floor and started praying. I asked the Lord to show me what was meant by those words, and the thoughts came.

"I call all people to come to Me. Some choose to do so. Many do not. For those who choose to choose Me, I call to follow Me. By that I mean to serve Me, to be used in ministry, however I call. Many say they choose Me, few actually follow Me, serving in joy. That is why I say 'the harvest is ripe, the laborers are few.' Commitment demands self sacrifice. Few are willing, yet I call. Pray my people hear. Pray my people choose to follow, to serve. Lip service without heart service is only lukewarm. For my Word says my people should be on fire for Me, red hot—not lukewarm. I must be first."

Wow. Now do you think I could just make up that kind of direction? Nope. That isn't even the way I talk. When I read the words again, all these years later, I am so thankful that I am able to choose daily to serve the living almighty God. The sacrifices I make, such as reading the newspaper later or not watching R-rated movies or not telling off color jokes, watching my language, are nothing compared to the joy that is poured into my being as I spend time each day focusing on the Lord. It is worth all the inconsequential things I always associated with being fun, being put aside. Do I laugh?

Yes, I do—a lot. Do I still enjoy jokes? Yes, but there can be funny jokes that are not off color or racist in content. Do

I still read the newspaper? Yes, at different times of the day or evening. It just depends, and it no longer seems so important. Do I watch movies? Oh, yes, but I am careful to listen to my inner spirit that nudges me if the content is something I should not watch. I love to read mysteries and romances, but again I listen to my inner spirit, and if I start feeling uncomfortable about the book, I don't read it.

Do I hunger for the old ways? No, not at all. In fact, if I were asked to evaluate myself today vs. twenty years ago, I believe I am a much more compassionate person. Certainly I have changed a lot in my attitudes. But before you think, *Oh, this woman really has it together,* don't despair. I continually learn—every day—more things the Lord would have me give up or change about myself. It is a constant process but one that is also an encouragement. I never feel that God gives up on teaching me or bringing to my mind things I need to repent of from years ago. And the interesting thing about bringing things to my mind is that God never does this until it seems I am ready to accept without allowing guilty feelings to hang on afterwards.

I share these things with you to hopefully draw you into a deeper relationship with Jesus. I pray that you will hear His call on your life and that you will serve Him eagerly and with joy. I pray most of all that through reading this book you will begin to realize how much God loves you, just as He does me. I want to share another prose poem given to me one morning during a vacation to the Outer Banks in August 1996. I was sitting on the deck of the beach house early in the morning, praying and basking in the moment.

"Loving Me"

One can walk through life believing they love Me, but
not really knowing Me.
One can speak my name with respect, yet not know me
deep in their hearts.

One can praise me with uplifted hands, yet not trust
that I am truly sovereign.

My little ones, hear your Father.
I watch your struggles, I see your temptations.
I feel your pain, I weep over your unwise choices.
Allow Me to be the focus of your life.
Allow Me to be the strength you hold on to.
Allow Me to be the buffer in relationships.
Do you not know there is nothing in the world
You can touch or see or feel
That can equal the deep abiding love I have for each
of you?

Salvation in Me you have,
But there is so much more I have waiting for each of
you.
I wait and wait. My angels hover.
My spirit is ready to fill you to overflowing.
Goodness, mercy, and praise,
Joy and laughter, gentleness and compassion.
Are all yours when you allow Me to fill you.
When you allow Me to be in control.

Surrender your heart as well as your mind to your Father
in heaven.
Feel the glory of God soaking into your very bones.
Be lifted out of your troubles into the secret places only
I can take you.
Worship Me, praise Me, and love Me. Me, not the
world.
Me, not things. Me, not emotions. Me, not power.
And I will give you life in abundance.

Written Aug. 16, 1996

Early in 1993 I began to wonder more and more what God's will was for me. Finally I asked Jim Donovan, one of the fellowship of our church who had been such an encouragement in my trusting in Jesus, "Just what is God's will? How do I know it is God's will and not mine?" Ha! Do you think he was kind enough to answer, because he knew? No. He said. "Start searching the Word, Evelyn. The Holy Spirit will point out very specifically God's will for you, and you will have no doubt, ever, about the answer to your question." *Great,* I thought, *another challenge.* As if I hadn't been challenged over and over the last fourteen years to dig into what was God's truth.

But I started listening to comments people made about God's will for their lives. I looked to see how people responded to the directions they believed were guidelines from the Lord. I read some books about God's will for us. Finally, in 1994, I started digging into the Bible, looking up all I could about God's will for us as believers in Christ Jesus. Eventually I came up with a list of desires God has for us. I have come to believe this list covers my question of God's will for me exceedingly well. A challenge for me to try, and I say try, each day to achieve at least one of these areas of the list.

We are to be lights to the world. (Eph. 5:8-11; Phil. 2:12-15)

We are to make the most of our days. (Matt. 7:25-34; Eph. 5:15-17)

We are not to be conformed to this world. (Rom. 12:2)

We are to become children of God. (1 John 3:1; John 1:12-13)

We are to honor Jesus. (John 5:22-23; Rev. 5:13)

We are to love one another as Jesus loves us. (John 13:34; 1 Corin. 13)

We are to serve God willingly and worship Him. (1 Pet. 5:2; Heb. 12:28)

We are to honor authority. (1 Pet. 2:13-15)

We are to be holy as God is holy. (1 Pet. 1:15-16)

We are to carry out Jesus' rescue mission. (Eph. 1:3-14 and 5:1-2)

God does not want anyone to perish, but to have eternal life with Him. (John 3:16; 2 Pet. 3:9)

Of course, there are many more references, but when I made up this list it blew my mind. This is certainly a clear directional map of how God wants me to live and to be in His will. But how could I do all this? The answer goes right back to realizing God made this world and all its complexities. Since it is complex, why should I not think that to do God's will is also difficult? Not a simple task put before me, but a new challenge. Why is it complex? Because we have to explore what our desires are versus what has been revealed to us as God's desire for us. Remember, Jesus knew we could not fulfill God's will for us when He left. That is exactly why we were given the Holy Spirit to guide us and teach us. Did you ever start to do something and have a nagging feeling that you shouldn't do it? The world would say that is probably our conscience. But when we are believers in Jesus, then we realize this is the Holy Spirit giving us a heightened awareness that we should stop and think about what we are planning to do. Often we ignore these feelings, usually to our sorrow. I have come to understand and believe deeply that the Holy Spirit is my guide to knowing God's will for me. Being obedient to God's will for us is not always easy. The simple way of life is to stand back and let others make the decisions for us. Then we can say, "Well it was just fate, or just luck." But there is the choice always.

Our Lord created us with free will. We have the choice in everything we do: The easy way, the fun way, the world's way, or God's way. I believe that praying to be guided by the Holy Spirit to do God's way, His will, in the long run causes us to be filled with a deep sense of joy. So how can you do this?

You can begin by choosing to turn off the TV for one half hour or hour during your leisure time and instead read about the Lord or meditate or pray. Thus begins the act of disciplining ourselves to seek God's will in our lives. There are so many good books available on prayer and how to listen to God and helps for trusting more in Him. Listen to Christian praise music. It lifts the soul and fills the very air around you with a deepening sense of God's presence. Read a few verses of scripture and think about what you have read, think how it could apply to your life. Any of these ways enlarge our understanding, our knowledge of who God is. It deepens our relationship with Jesus. It opens us up to a heightened awareness of the Holy Spirit working in us. The more we communicate with the Lord, the more we seek knowledge, the closer we come to Him, and the more we will desire to do His will. There will be a clearer understanding of His will for us, and I can promise you that joy will be there. Also there is a peace that floods our very being. It radiates from head to toe and carries us through trials. It enables us to withstand suffering. It illuminates and grows our spirit. In other words, drawing closer to the Lord, seeking His will in our lives, allows each day to be even better than the day before.

In 1 John 5:14-15 it says, "This is the confidence we have in approaching God: that if we ask anything according to his will, he hears us. And if we know that he hears us—whatever we ask—we know that we have what we asked of him."

What does this scripture tell us about prayer and about God's will for us? We are to pray with confidence. Why? Because God hears our prayers and promises to give us whatever we ask. However there is a stipulation that people often ignore, then say, "I asked God for....but He didn't hear me." We are to ask ACCORDING TO HIS WILL. Whoa. Doesn't that make a big difference in our asking for something in prayer? God's will is for us to ask for the things He knows we really need, things that are good for us. What are these things that are good for us? Remember we are to be conformed to the likeness of Jesus. We are to be given or filled with wisdom, understanding, virtue, love, joy, godliness, prayerfulness, compassion, a serving heart, and a desire to put God first in our lives. Now let's face it. Do most of us ask God for these things in our prayers? I expect it is usually for financial gain, marital bliss, having our own way, changing the viewpoint or actions of another person, taking away a problem, health issues, happiness, etc.

In understanding how to pray according to God's will, it is good to think about from whom we are seeking help. This is our Heavenly Father, the living God, the God who was and is to come. The God who never changes. The God who is all-powerful, all-knowledgeable and yet the God who loves us with an everlasting love. So when we communicate with God, we don't demand what we want or how we want it done. He already knows the best plan. We discuss with God what He wants for us. We always thank Him even in the midst of our troubles, acknowledging that God knows better than we what is truly best for us. Our God is faithful and has promised to see us through our problems even though He may not take the problems away. There have been situations I have put before the Lord that He resolved in ways I would not have expected, but in looking back I can see the overall good that came from the way the Lord resolved it. It took me a long time to understand that God can see the big picture. He withholds answers until just the right time.

An example might be we pray for a man's healing. The healing does not come, but the man's faith is increased. His wife comes to know and accept Jesus. The family is united and bonded together in this illness. Thus God answered the prayer beyond what was asked. Sometimes God answers prayers by creating opportunities or opening doors. He does this in love. And then we choose. God does not intervene in choice. He has given every person free will. But will the person grab the opportunity to go through the door, trusting in God's wisdom? This is why it is so important to study the Word. It helps us to trust in God, to release ourselves to His control, to have faith in waiting, in believing God really truly cares about every single situation we face.

There is nothing that we cannot bring to the Lord that He does not already know, even the things we think we have hidden. But he loves us so much, He desires for us to face all wants, problems, and hurts so that in His perfect will we can be released. Isn't that a special blessing? As we seek the Lord's will, the abundant life promised us by the cross becomes more evident. When we take time to sit in the presence of the Lord and pray, then we are opening our hearts to surrender to Him. Jesus gave us the example of the "oneness" He had with the Father through prayer (John 17:13-23) and Jesus desired this for all believers. The blessings from the Lord are waiting for us, but we must desire them and ask for them. The whole nature and glory of God's blessings consist of being obtained in answer to prayer by hearts entirely surrendered to the Lord and by hearts that believe in the power of prayer. We do not have to be perfect in order to come before the Lord in prayer. We do not have to wait until we have our lives in order to come before the Lord. Jesus said He longed greatly to pour His love into our hearts, so that we, in the consciousness of weakness, could confidently rely on Him to bestow the grace of prayer. Such a beautiful promise!

Our whole relationship with the Lord becomes a new thing as we strive to enter into a different way of asking and expecting answers to prayer. We must believe in God's infinite love. We must believe in His divine power. We must believe in Jesus who, as the great intercessor, through the Holy Spirit, will inspire each of us with joy and power for communion with our Heavenly

Father in prayer. When we desire this—really desire this—do you know what is going to happen to you?

For perhaps the first time, prayer will become what it really is—the natural and joyous breathing of the spiritual life by which the heavenly atmosphere is inhaled and then exhaled in prayer. Our relationship with the Lord will become a focal point in our daily living. For some, this experience might happen right away, for others it will be a growing experience. For me, it started with a desire to pray but not knowing how. I thought I could never pray for a long time. I figured I could pray for those I knew, but how could I pray for those I did not know? How could I pray for longer than five or ten minutes? Know what I found out? God takes care of all those questions. Just as Scripture promises, when we do not know how to pray, the Spirit takes over for us. We reach the place where we desire to pray more and more. There is a hunger to be in the presence of the Almighty God. There is a need to draw upon His strength. There is a special comfort in just basking in His presence. There is a joy that fills our very being no matter what the situation. His peace truly passes all understanding. This is the peace that floods our very being. It radiates from head to toe and carries us through trials. It enables us to withstand suffering and illuminates and grows our spirit. Have I said this before? Probably, but at least for me, this understanding has had such an impact on my life, I wanted to stress the wonderful reward our Lord blesses us with when we seek Him.

In order for us to become people of prayer—that is, praying for others as intercessors or prayer warriors, we first have to come to an understanding of our own prayer lives. When we question, when we fail, when we goof—and we surely will—there is always the opportunity to confess and repent and turn the situation over to the Lord to begin anew. Our desire to serve our Lord even more willingly in more humility and, yes, in more excitement, becomes imbedded in our hearts. I used the word "excitement." I think there is much excitement in uncovering what it is that God will do through each of us. It is exciting to see a person commit his or her life and watch God just take over. Perhaps our prayers have helped. Perhaps our sincerity in trusting the Lord and expressing that trust in our daily living helped in encouraging another person to seek what we have. It is said there is much power in prayer, and I do believe this. The power is not ours. The power is released by the Holy Spirit in us and through us as we pray for another. We know God's Holy Word is true. Therefore we must believe in it without doubt. This belief or trust has to be strong enough that when prayers are lifted up for other people we believe God is able to do all things. We believe God will break down walls. He will remove evil spirits. He will heal physical and psychological symptoms. We must truly recognize and believe God *is*. He is the very God of all. There is no glory for us, only for the Lord. There is absolutely no way we can have this power in our own strength. Actually, we would just mess it up, wouldn't we? Our pride would no doubt get in the way. We might begin to think, "look at me" or "look at what I can do" or feel superior to others. We must remember that any miracle of healing, any answers to our prayers is the doing of the Lord. We are simply the vessels the Holy Spirit uses at that moment. I encourage you to always give the glory to God and the praise to Jesus and thankfulness to the inspiration of the Holy Spirit. I have found a great freedom in realizing I do not have to resolve a situation or have answers to problems or to be all knowledgeable. All I am required to do is pray in love for the person asking for prayer and believe God is able. This has given me a great joy in praying for others, even when they do not know I have been praying for them. Again—God getting the glory.

Reader, if any of this has encouraged you, or if any of this has tugged at your heart to deepen your prayer life and you promise yourself to work on it, do you know what I believe will happen?

As your prayer life becomes more and more your daily desire, lives will be changed. Healings will take place. Faith in the Lord will be established on a deeper level. People will seek you for prayer and assurances. The desire to know Jesus will be contagious. You will find yourself with a hunger to witness the love of Jesus. This then is the beginning of the release of God's power in prayer. Exciting? Yes. Humbling? Yes. Joyful? Oh, yes.

CHAPTER 14

A Christian Woman's Grief

So far I have been sharing with you, dear reader, my wonderful relationship with the Lord and how it has affected every area of my life over the past twenty-four years. But I could not finish this book without sharing about the love affair I had with my husband of so many years. Bill—just an ordinary guy, but how he loved me! All of our married life he showered me with protection, compliments, love, and encouragement. He spoiled me terribly, and I loved every minute of it. Yes, I took it for granted much of the time. We certainly had our share of fights, but what fun to make up. He thought I was beautiful—I'm not; but in his eyes I was. He thought I was really smart and often said I could do anything I wanted. Again, I believe I have just the usual intelligence, but he always encouraged me to strive for whatever goal I desired, believing in me. He worked hard all his life to give me everything he could. He was a carpenter and model maker of jet engines. We raised six children, lots of times arguing over the correct method of discipline, but there was always love behind the actions and disciplines. There was joy in seeing the children grow up to be caring adults. Could any woman want more?

When I started writing this book in 1997, I never dreamed I would be writing a chapter on death. So many times as people grow older and the kids leave home, the husband and wife grow apart. But for Bill and me, it became a time to grow closer, each doing what we really enjoyed, giving the other freedom to focus on his or her own special interests. Yet our times together were so much fun. We loved walking on beaches, playing golf, eating out, being with friends, family gatherings, talking about the Lord, sharing comments about TV programs, traveling to new places. Simple things? Yes, but that, I believe, is what true deep love is all about.

On Super Bowl weekend, January 1998, Bill became very sick. It seemed more than flu, and by Sunday night he could not even walk to his chair, he crawled to it. I insisted on taking him to the doctor on Monday. Eventually he was diagnosed with polymyalgia rheumatica with serious complications of temporal arteritis. This is supposedly a self-limiting disease that goes away within one to two years with treatment. After two years of massive amounts of medication, some even experimental, and tests and more tests, going to the Cleveland Clinic, and seeing numerous doctors, my dear husband died on February 9, 2000.

I want to share with you a little of how I saw our Lord working in the last four weeks of his life as he lay in the ICU of the hospital. The first day I took him to the emergency room he was not expected to live through the night. Yet our Lord watched over him and protected him until all three girls could fly here from their homes around the country to say their final goodbyes. My three sons were so faithful in being at the hospital every single day to encourage their dad and to support me. The doctors were astounded that Bill seemed to be fighting so hard and making headway with a greatly compromised immune system. Yet in my heart I just knew he was never coming home. Bill was in a drug-induced coma and had a tracheotomy tube inserted for breathing, so he was not able to communicate.

Some days I took my Bible to the hospital and read verses to him. Pastor Mike came and prayed with him often. The ministers from my daughter, Mary Evelyn's, Lutheran church visited and prayed with Bill. The priest and deacon from Bill's Roman Catholic Church prayed with him occasionally. The nursing staff, which changed frequently, were all so kind and comforting. There was such a peace felt in his room and tears were not shed much, just love expressed by all the children for their dad. When a person is in a drug-induced coma or upon awakening (which he did for two days) but unable to speak, that person cannot respond except by squeezing your hand or fluttering his eyelids or turning his head. Because of this inability to communicate in a normal way, much that one would like to say is not said. I just stood by his bed and prayed and waited and watched and hoped and remembered.

One day while I was at home during his hospital stay, I knelt on the floor and cried out to God to heal my husband, to make him like he had been two years before. I was sobbing so hard, and yet deep down I knew that my prayer was not going to be answered the way I wanted it to be. I sensed it was time for me to relinquish Bill to the complete healing that only our God can give. So I did that. I asked the Lord to give me strength to get through these weeks, to help me believe God knew best, and to just thank Him every day for the gift of Bill in my life. I told the Lord if it was Bill's time to go home with Him, then I would accept that. I asked the Lord to give me peace about Bill's death. I asked Him to help me be a role model of trust for my children throughout this ordeal. Such peace poured over me and into me. It carried me through every single day of those final weeks. I saw the love of Jesus in the faces of so many friends, ministers, nursing staff, doctors, and even the cleaning people. Every single person I came into contact with at that hospital was so supportive. And goodness, how faithful were my friends in praying for our family.

On Tuesday evening of the fourth week, the doctor called me at home and said I needed to make a decision on how far they should go in keeping Bill alive on machines. Bill and I had talked about living on machines and had drawn up Living Wills years before, so I knew heroic efforts were not what Bill wanted. Wednesday morning all three sons met with me at the hospital. I gave the release stating that if Bill's heart stopped then it was because the Lord was calling him home, therefore no efforts were to be made to keep him breathing by a machine. Around 10:00 A.M. the doctor said it was only a matter of twenty-four to thirty-six hours because all Bill's vital organs were shutting down. I went into his room and touched his leg—it was ice cold. The nurse explained the capillaries were shutting down in his legs already. Pastor Mike came and prayed over Bill. My son, Patrick, called his dad's church and the priest came over and gave the last rites to Bill. A short time later, Rev. Tom Sweets from my church came and said another prayer over Bill. Around one o'clock in the afternoon my dear friend, Lucille (I have mentioned her earlier) came. She cannot drive because of her eyes, and a friend of hers who lived in another town came all the way to Lucille's home to bring her to the hospital. Lucille is an intercessor and a burden had been put on her heart all morning that she must come—not knowing that Bill was dying. She prayed and prayed and said to me, "I keep thinking about angels, about them singing, but am not sure how to pray." I told her Bill had sung in the choir at his church and one of his favorite songs was "This Little Light of Mine." Lucille said, "Oh, I know that song," and she sang it. We both saw Bill's eyelids flutter. After she left and it was getting to be late afternoon, I was agonizing over whether to go home for a while and come back. I was running the ideas by my son, Ken. He was standing by Bill's bed and suddenly said, "Mom, something's going on." The monitors were going crazy and I ran to get the nurse, just as she was coming in. I asked, "What is it?" She replied,

"He is trying to die." We were all around his bed as he took his last breath. I have to tell you about my impression of his dying. It was beautiful. I sensed calm, peace, poignant quietness, and felt the presence of the Lord so strongly. There was no struggling on Bill's part. No grasping at the blanket or tossing his head back and forth; just a sigh, a few gulping breaths, and then his head dropping to the side. I knew without a doubt Bill's spirit was soaring high into the heavens to be with our Lord. So ended my marriage at 4:30 P.M. that Wednesday afternoon.

Did you notice anything unusual about the visitors praying for my husband that last day? There were two pastors from a Presbyterian Church, a priest from a Roman Catholic Church, and an intercessor from a Pentecostal Church. And I was later informed that the minister from my daughter, Mary Evelyn's, Lutheran church was standing outside as Bill was dying but did not want to intrude. As soon as my third son, Tom, got to the hospital from his work and said his goodbyes to his dad, Patrick asked me to pray with all the family. We formed a circle by Bill's bed. The hospital chaplain was there and several of the nurses asked to join us. As I prayed, I thanked God for Bill's life and how he had been a faithful husband and a loving father.

As I thought about that day later, I realized how Bill's illness had shown us how our love in Christ Jesus reaches out in unity to encircle God's children at a time of crisis when we are not putting up barriers. A very good thing. The nurses commented they had never seen such a peaceful and beautiful death.

I next entered a whole new world. I never knew that when your loved one died you were not considered married any longer but considered a single person. I discovered that when I was filling out forms for changing financial accounts. Everywhere I went, I was so aware of twosomes. I found out over and over how much Bill had done for me around the house—putting air in the tires, checking the furnace, dragging out the garbage cans, digging out old bushes. Let me tell you, cooking for one is not fun. Hundreds of little things that we all take for granted reached out and caught me unaware and caused me to feel an incredible sadness. Even now, years later, there is still this incredible sadness—the longing and missing the closeness of my husband.

What I have learned about grieving, however, is that right from the very day you lose a loved one, there are absolutely no words that will really comfort. Words you don't want to hear, "Oh, he is better off, his suffering is over." That is not comforting. Of course, I knew he was better off. My tears were not for Bill. God answered our prayers for healing in the most complete healing of all, taking Bill to be home with Him. Bill is fine. But my tears were for me, for my utter aloneness, for all the things I wish I had said more often. For not ever being able again to feel his hugs or hear his compliments or his encouraging words, for sharing the joy together in our children's accomplishments. For not being together in a crowd, catching his eye, and knowing we were thinking the same thing. Again, the little things.

Another phrase people say, "You were lucky to have him for so long." Well, that is not helpful or consoling. Two years, ten years, twenty years, more or less—it is all relative. If you have something good going, you want it to continue forever. People pat you on the arm and say, "It will get easier." Not true. You just get more used to being alone. Then there are the people who say, "Call me if I can be of help." Right, I'm going to call and ask some woman's husband to come and fix a household problem? It doesn't happen. I am fortunate to have three sons who are willing to help me out when I do have a problem that I can't figure out. Instead of those eight little words said during the deep grieving time, how nice it would be to have a call occasionally offering an hour or two. Gosh, ladies, come with your husband and visit with the grieving widow. Bring a little plant or a small plate of cookies. Give the person a hug. Show you care. Talk about the person who is dead, remembering anything you can about him. About two months after the death, reality hits home and you realize this is permanent. It is not going away.

So what should a person say to someone who is grieving? I believe the very best thing a person can do is just give you a hug. Perhaps say, "I am so sorry" or "I'm praying for God's comfort for you." In this last case, please say it only if you really are praying.

Another thing I have noticed is that after the initial first few weeks of grieving, many people never seem comfortable mentioning the deceased person's name. It's as if they are afraid you will cry or something. What's wrong with allowing tears to well up? Denying that Bill ever lived is the most hurtful thing I have had to deal with. It is helpful to remember the funny things he said or the silly quirks he had. If you want to comfort someone, just mention the loved one's name and allow the person to share remembrances for a little while. Even if they have shared it with you before, be patient as this is a gift you are giving the one who is grieving. With my sons and daughters we talk about Bill a lot. We laugh at some of the things that happened over the years. We shed tears. We hug—a lot. And yes, I do have friends who know how to comfort, especially those who have been through this themselves. That is why I am sharing this. Not to complain about those who were only trying to comfort but just didn't know how—but to give you suggestions for the next time you are confronted with a similar situation.

Through all of this, my leaning on the strength and comfort of the Lord has deepened and deepened. He is such a faithful God. I have seen my children draw closer to God through the death of their father. I could have become angry that God did not heal Bill of this supposedly simple disease, but all along I just kept walking the walk of faith, one day at a time. I am still doing this. Sometimes it is one hour at a time. Some days, hours go by before the aloneness hits me. But I know without a doubt that my God is a God of love. He sees my grief, He sees my tears, He hears my cries, and He comforts. Every so often when I have a "bad day" as I call it, the phone rings and someone is calling to say, "I was just thinking about you." How that comforts. How that ministers. When you feel the urge, never hesitate to make that phone call. You don't have to have a whole bunch of words of wisdom. I doubt most people are looking for that. There is comfort in knowing that someone cared enough to call. A touch or a hug means so much when you see a person who is grieving. When a person is alone, the touching is sorely missed.

I don't imagine there is any set time or limit to how long a person grieves. I can't speak to grieving the loss of a child, but I would think that it must be a different kind of grief, a longing that will always be with a parent for that child who was once a part of him or her. Again, I can't speak for a husband's grief and what he faces and the best way to deal with it. But I do believe, from my experience, that God is always with us, willing to comfort us, to help us through this difficult and grieving process.

Throughout this book I have mentioned seeking God in prayer. Sometimes during this grieving period my prayers were really just talking to God. Through my tears, my sobbing, I have said, "God, I hate this. Make it go away. I want Bill back." I know, of course, that is impossible, but I also believe God wants me to lean on Him and to express my innermost thoughts. It is at those very moments I often feel His presence so much. The tears stop. I wipe my eyes and go on. Sometimes God floods my mind with beautiful memories and then the tears are ones of sweet remembrance.

So grief can be part of our walk with Jesus. I have heard this phrase used many times over the years as part of the Christian jargon. "You have to walk the walk, or walk the talk." Many times I questioned what that means. For me, that walking the walk is part of the faith that we are given by the Holy Spirit that sustains us through times of grief, difficulties, problems, and fears. When we choose to walk the walk with our Lord, we treasure our memories of the good times, release the memories of the bad times. We don't worry so much about tomorrow, simply trusting that God is able to help us deal with tomorrow when it comes. We just focus on today. This day. Right now. Sometimes it is so hard that it is just this moment or just this hour. But we are promised by the words of Scripture that our God will never leave us or forsake us. He loves us with an everlasting love. Nothing is hidden from Him. He knows every single thing that happens to us.

I treasure these promises. I thank our Father every day that He does love me. I ask for comfort and guidance every morning. I thank and praise Him for who He is, mighty God, everlasting Rock, and my sure foundation. He is the foundation of the road that I want to walk for the rest of my life. I cannot imagine getting through this time any other way. For this walk continually brings me to a place where I can experience the contentment and the joy of the Lord in all things. Yes, in all things, even in my grief.

CHAPTER 15

Whenever I think about how much God loves me, I am just naturally drawn to the final days of the life of Jesus. In Max Lucado's book, *And the Angels Were Silent,* he draws the reader into the walk that Jesus took each day of that final week. From that book it was impressed upon my heart the finality, the never-swerving focus Jesus had for all of us. As he walked from Jericho to Jerusalem, His stride was purposeful and confident. He led the procession of believers and no doubt curiosity seekers that were with Him. With each step that drew Him closer to Jerusalem, I wonder if His heart became heavier and heavier. We know He stopped and wept over the city. We know that the people were expecting a glorious, powerful king when the Messiah came. Yet Jesus entered Jerusalem on a lowly donkey.

As cries went forth, "Hail to the Messiah!" "Hail to the king!" "Blessed is He who comes in the name of the Lord!" I wonder if Jesus could hear in His mind the kind of cries that would be thrown at Him just a few days later. Scripture tells us Jesus performed no more miracles upon entering Jerusalem. The signs and wonders ceased for the multitudes. He seemed to feel the necessity to fill the time with teaching, with examples to fill

His disciples with as much truth as He could in those last days. He explained why He must die. He washed the disciples feet to show His humility, the full extent of His love them. He shared the Last Supper with them.

I try to put myself in the position of sharing a last meal with the ones I love most. What would be my thoughts, my reactions?

I treasure the smiles, the meeting of eyes, and the camaraderie. There is sadness in my heart as I think about leaving them. I want to warn them about all that could happen if they are not watchful. I want to encourage them. No, just straight out tell them the Lord is their strength. But deep down, I know they will listen to only so much. They will absorb only so much. They cannot believe I am leaving. They wonder how I could possibly know that I am leaving. I touch each one, feeling the warmth of his or her hand, or shoulder or cheek. In my mind I say a prayer for each one, Lord, keep him safe. May your Holy Spirit convict her to know you deeply, surely. Fill him with encouragement, strength, wisdom, and insight. And inside my heart I am crying out, I don't want to leave them. They need me. They are part of me. There is so much more I could tell them.

Alas, I am only human. It is impossible for me to understand what Jesus must have been feeling, but apparently there was much anguish in His prayers to the Father that last week. We know He went into the garden, the disciples with Him. At that late hour He prayed and prayed. Yet Jesus understood that He must obey the will of His Father. How often do we pray for our wants and not our needs when actually our needs, especially the need to be in a close relationship with Jesus, should be our prayer? Have we ever prayed so earnestly that we have sweat blood? What love Jesus has for us.

I am going to skip over the next few days and go right to that dark Friday. At this point Jesus is up on the cross. Some of those who cried out "Crucify him, Crucify him!" were no doubt standing under the cross, watching the scene. They could see Him suffer, and yet His final words were to comfort others, His mother, a criminal on the cross, those who crucified Him. Is that not a love far beyond the conditional love we give to people?

At the sixth hour, darkness came over the whole land (Mark 15:33), and at the ninth hour Jesus breathed His last. Now those who had followed Him were watching from a distance. The curtain of the temple was torn in two from top to bottom. If the sun was covered up it must have been very dark. Yet the centurion who stood in front of the cross heard Jesus cry out and saw how He died. His words were, "Surely this man was the Son of God" (Mark 15:39).

In Luke 23:48 we are told, "When all the people who had gathered to witness this sight saw what took place, they beat their breasts and went away." What did they see?

I recently watched a video given by Ed Silvoso on "Revival and Spiritual Warfare For Our Cities." I was ironing as I watched and listened. He brought the above picture out and asked the question, "What did they see?" This grabbed my attention. I just stopped ironing, turned off the video, and sat on the floor with my Bible. I began reading Mark's and Luke's accounts of the crucifixion. All of a sudden I was weeping and praying, and I asked God, "Lord, what did they see? Was it a light around Jesus? Was it just a sense of your presence, a powerful silence? Was it just a brightness? What caused them to walk away beating their breasts when all was dark?" And then I remembered vaguely, Ed Silvoso had mentioned something about 2 Corinthians. "Where is it Lord?" I cried out. I was still weeping, not understanding but feeling driven to find the answer. It came to me as I looked at 2 Corinthians 4. There it was in verse 6. "For God, who said, 'Let light shine out of darkness' made his light shine in our hearts to give us the light of the knowledge of the glory of God in the face of Jesus."

That was it. I believe this must be what the people saw—the glory of God on the face of Jesus. No wonder they went away beating their breasts. Perhaps they were convicted to ask themselves, *What have we done?* The centurion knew. I wonder how those people's lives were changed. What a revelation that morning was for me. How alive the words of scripture become when we pray and ask God to give us wisdom and understanding. Every year during Lent I think about the people, the darkness, the terrible silence, and then the mutterings and wailing of those who loved Jesus, not knowing then that Jesus would be with them forever.

One thing I know without a shadow of a doubt. Jesus was and is and will always be the beloved Son of God. He was born, died, and resurrected for me. Because He willingly, lovingly, stretched out His arms on a cross, Jesus became my bridge to eternity. My sins are forgiven. God's grace has promised me salvation. I will be with the Father forever. God loves me so.

Dear reader, has this account of what I discovered about Jesus, the Holy Spirit, and our Heavenly Father stirred a longing in your heart to experience the same? Believe me, the results of what I have just shared with you about my experiences for the past twenty-some years are not just for me alone, but for you also. I pray that you too will know, without a shadow of doubt, Jesus was and is and will always be the beloved Son of God. He was born, died, and resurrected for each of you. Because He willingly, lovingly, stretched out His arms on a cross, Jesus became your bridge to eternity. When you accept Jesus into your life, your sins are forgiven. God's grace has promised you salvation. You will be with the Father forever. You will experience joy that wells up from inside and bubbles over into all your daily living. I pray you start the journey. Each step will be a promise of more delights to come because God loves you so.

I pray that the words given me as I prepared to write this book will be fulfilled beyond my wildest expectations. The promise was; "This book is to be a fresh wind blowing into the hearts of people. For God says, 'I control the wind of the Spirit and when and where I want it to fall onto the face and into the heart of the people, it will." I also pray that every word written, every thought I expressed with regard to my understanding of God's love, adheres to Scripture. All the glory, all the praise I give to the Father, Son, and Holy Spirit. It was only by God's faithfulness in helping me and encouraging me, and, yes, at times, reminding me, that I have finally been able to finish this book. It took me "only" seven years to trust that God could and would help me put together all the thoughts and notes and journaling from the beginning of my "growing in God." And best of all, dear reader, I have the promise that God will continue to grow me. Each time I step out in faith into a new area of serving, each time I teach a new Bible study, each time I earnestly seek help in prayer, our dear, faithful Lord grows me a little more.

May it be the same for each of you.

About the Author

Evelyn McCarthy is a widow with six grown children. She has fifteen grandchildren. She lives in Cincinnati, Ohio. Evelyn is active in her church serving in leadership capacity and chairing ministries involving worship and prayer.

For a number of years Evelyn has written monthly prayer articles for the newsletter of the large church membership. For the past five years she has written stories for the annual Women's Advent Program. On occasion Evelyn has spoken to groups about the life of prayer.

She enjoys painting in watercolor, bridge, golf, and is an avid NASCAR fan. This is her first venture into the world of writing and publishing a book.

To order additional copies of

Have your credit card ready and call:

1-877-421-READ (7323)

or please visit our web site at
www.pleasantword.com

Also available at:
www.amazon.com
and
www.barnesandnoble.com

Printed in the United States
54987LVS00002B/1-144

9 781414 106366